Dinosaurs!

A supplement to
Childcraft—The How and Why Library

World Book, Inc.

a Scott Fetzer company

Chicago London Sydney Toronto

Contents

Preface

Less than two hundred years ago, no one ever dreamed there was such a thing as a dinosaur. Today, everyone knows about dinosaurs. They are especially popular with children. Even young children who can barely write their own names are often familiar with such dinosaur names as *Tyrannosaurus, Stegosaurus,* and *Triceratops.*

In recent years, we have learned more and more about dinosaurs. At one time, we thought that most dinosaurs plodded along, dragging their tails. We now know that most of them held their tails up off the ground, and that many could move very quickly. It was once thought that all dinosaurs were cold-blooded, like modern reptiles, but most scientists now think many dinosaurs were warm-blooded, like birds and mammals. There are new ideas about what caused the extinction of the dinosaurs, and even an idea that birds are descendants of the dinosaurs.

This book presents the latest available scientific information about dinosaurs. Here, then, is what scientists now know for sure, and what they believe, about more than seventy of those exciting animals of long ago, the dinosaurs!

Learning
About
Dinosaurs

The discovery of dinosaurs

People have known of dinosaurs for only about 150 years. Before then, no one dreamed there had ever been such creatures. The word *dinosaur* (DY nuh sawr) didn't even exist. Anyone who chanced to dig up a fossil (preserved) dinosaur bone or tooth might have thought it had come from an elephant —or perhaps from a dragon or a giant! There were few if any people who could look at a bone and tell what sort of animal it had come from.

But by 150 years ago there were a good many scientists who could examine a bone or tooth and tell exactly what kind of animal it had come from. Some of these men were very interested in the fossil remains of ancient animals. And they began to discover a number of fossils that they knew had come from reptiles—scaly skinned creatures such as lizards, snakes, and crocodiles. But most reptiles of today are rather small, and these fossil reptile bones and teeth were enormous!

In a book written in 1824, an Englishman named William Buckland described a huge fossil jaw that had been dug up near an English town. He was sure it had come from some kind of gigantic meat-eating reptile that had lived long ago, but was no longer around. He called this creature *Megalosaurus* (mehg uh loh SAWR uhs), which means "giant lizard." It was the first dinosaur to be named.

In 1825, another Englishman, Gideon Mantell, wrote about some fossil teeth his wife had found three years earlier. They were like the teeth of lizards called iguanas, but much, much bigger. Mantell believed the teeth must have come from some kind of ancient giant iguana (ih GWAH nuh), so he called the creature *Iguanodon* (ih GWAHN uh dahn), which means "iguana tooth." *Iguanodon* was the second dinosaur to be named. But there still was no such word as *dinosaur*.

In 1822, Dr. Gideon Mantell and his wife found the huge fossil tooth (below) of the dinosaur *Iguanodon*.

During the next few years, fossils of other ancient giant reptiles were found and named. There were *Hylaeosaurus* (hy lee uh SAWR uhs), or "forest lizard," and *Cetiosaurus* (see tee uh SAWR uhs), or "whale lizard," in England, and *Plateosaurus* (plat ee uh SAWR uhs), or "flat lizard," in Germany. Scientists now realized that a great many different kinds of giant reptiles must have lived long ago.

A name was needed for these reptiles, just as there is a name for every other group of animals that are alike. In 1841, the English scientist Richard Owen suggested these huge, terrible-seeming reptiles should be called *dinosaurs*. The word is made up from the Greek words *deinos*, which means "terrible," and *sauros*, which means "lizard." And dinosaurs, or "terrible lizards," is what everyone began calling them. As it turned out, this really wasn't a very good name, because dinosaurs were *not* lizards.

These statues, made in 1851, show what
scientists first thought dinosaurs looked like.

So, dinosaurs had been discovered. But for some
time, scientists had only a few bones or teeth of
each creature. They still didn't have a very good
idea of what the different kinds of dinosaurs had
been like. They thought of them as simply looking
much like the lizards of today, only many times
bigger. In 1851, an artist made some statues
showing what scientists thought dinosaurs had
looked like. All the statues were fat-bodied,
four-legged, lizardlike beasts with big, blunt heads.

But then, in America, in the year 1858, an almost
complete skeleton of a dinosaur was dug up.

Scientists saw that this animal had not been a bit like a lizard or any other kind of reptile living now. They could tell that it must have walked upright on its two back legs, much like a kangaroo. They named it *Hadrosaurus* (had ruh SAWR uhs), meaning "bulky lizard."

As time went on, more and more whole skeletons of different kinds of dinosaurs were dug up. Scientists began to learn more and more about these ancient reptiles. Today, we know of more than eight hundred different kinds of dinosaurs. And we know that these reptiles weren't at all like any reptiles living today. Dinosaurs were a very special kind of creature.

What was a dinosaur?

Dinosaurs lived during a time we have named the Age of Reptiles, because so many different kinds of reptiles lived then. There were reptiles with wings, sea-dwelling reptiles, and land-dwelling reptiles. Many people think *all* these creatures were dinosaurs, but that's not correct. Dinosaurs were a very special kind of reptile, different from all others.

What made the dinosaurs different was the way their hips were formed and the way they stood and walked. A reptile such as a lizard or turtle stands with its legs sprawled out to the side and its body touching the ground. To move, it creeps along with its underside usually dragging on the ground. But a dinosaur stood and walked with its legs straight under its body, and its body held up off the ground.

The first kinds of dinosaurs probably all walked upright on their two back legs most of the time. Later, many kinds of dinosaurs had become so huge and heavy that they couldn't walk on two legs but needed all four to support their weight. Even so, they still walked with all four legs straight, holding their bodies well up off the ground, just as an elephant does.

Dinosaurs were also land animals—there were no sea-dwelling dinosaurs and no dinosaurs with wings. So, if anyone ever asks you what a dinosaur was, tell them that dinosaurs were all land-dwelling reptiles that walked with their legs straight and their bodies up off the ground. They were unlike most other kinds of reptiles that lived then or now. They were something quite special, and there's no reptile the least bit like them in the world today.

A phytosaur (FY tuh sawr), or "plant lizard," was a prehistoric reptile. Like most reptiles, it had sprawling legs.

Plateosaurus was one
kind of dinosaur.
Unlike most other kinds
of reptiles, dinosaurs
walked on straight legs.

The dinosaur families

Scientists have divided dinosaurs into two groups, or *orders*, according to the way their hipbones are formed. In one order, almost all the dinosaurs have hipbones somewhat like those of other kinds of reptiles, so they are known as saurischians (saw RIHS kee uhnz), or "lizard hips." In the other order, the dinosaurs have hipbones that are more like those of birds. They are known as ornithischians (awr nuh THIHS kee uhnz), or "bird hips."

Each of the two orders is made up of a number of dinosaur families. These are not families of a mother, father, and young ones; they are groups of animals that are all much alike. The cat family, for example, is made up of lions, tigers, leopards, pussycats, and many other creatures that are all much alike.

In the saurischian order there are nine families of bulky, four-legged, long-necked and long-tailed dinosaurs that ate plants. They are known as sauropods (SAWR uh pahdz), or "lizard feet" and prosauropods (proh SAWR uh pahdz), or "early lizard feet," because of the way their feet are shaped.

There are also ten families of two-legged dinosaurs that were mostly meat-eaters. These dinosaurs are known as theropods (THIHR uh pahdz), or "beast feet." The large and heavy theropods are called carnosaurs (KAHR nuh sawrz),

One dinosaur group *(left)* had hipbones like those of lizards. The other group *(right)* had hipbones like those of birds.

or "flesh lizards." The small theropods, which had hollow bones, are called coelurosaurs (suh LUHR uh sawrz), or "hollow-tailed lizards."

In the ornithischian order there are six families of two-legged plant-eating dinosaurs called ornithopods (awr NIHTH uh pahdz), or "bird feet." There are three families of ceratopsians (sehr uh TAHP see uhnz), or "horned faces," three families of ankylosaurs (an KY luh sawrz), or armored dinosaurs, and one family of stegosaurs (STEHG uh sawrz), or "roofed reptiles." Stegosaurs got their name because they had bony plates that looked like roof shingles sticking up out of their backs.

Each dinosaur family is divided into one or more groups. Each group is called a genus (JEE nuhs). All the animals in a genus are alike, but are different from those in every other genus.

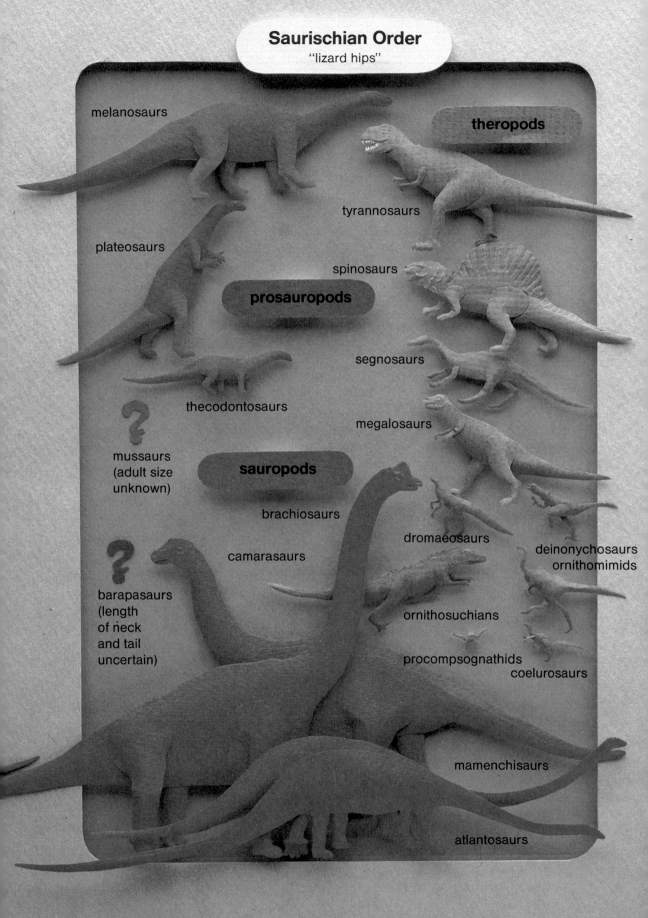

Saurischian Order
"lizard hips"

melanosaurs

theropods

tyrannosaurs

plateosaurs

spinosaurs

prosauropods

segnosaurs

thecodontosaurs

megalosaurs

mussaurs
(adult size
unknown)

sauropods

brachiosaurs

dromaeosaurs

camarasaurs

deinonychosaurs
ornithomimids

barapasaurs
(length
of neck
and tail
uncertain)

ornithosuchians

procompsognathids

coelurosaurs

mamenchisaurs

atlantosaurs

Ornithischian Order
"bird hips"

hadrosaurs

ornithopods

iguanodons

fabrosaurs

hypsilophodonts

pachycephalosaurs

heterodontosaurs

stegosaurs

stegosaurs

ankylosaurs

nodosaurs

ankylosaurs

scelidosaurs

ceratopsians

psittacosaurs

protoceratopsians

ceratopsians

How did dinosaurs get their names?

Pachycephalosaurus (pak uh SEHF uh loh sawr uhs). *Dromiceiomimus* (droh mih see oh MY muhs). *Compsognathus* (kahmp suh NAY thus). Most dinosaur names are real tongue twisters. Why is that?

The person who discovers a new kind of dinosaur is entitled to name it. Usually, of course, that person is a scientist. Scientists all over the world long ago agreed that any kind of newly discovered animal, whether living or extinct, must be given a scientific name. The name is usually made up from words taken from Greek or Latin, languages with which most scientists are familiar. Thus a newly discovered dinosaur gets a name that scientists can understand, no matter what language they speak.

The name usually tells something about the dinosaur. For example, when one scientist discovered a dinosaur that had a large, curved, sharp claw on each hind foot, he named the dinosaur *Deinonychus* (dy noh NIHK uhs), or "terrible claw." Or, the name may simply tell where the fossil was found. A dinosaur whose skeleton was found in Shantung, China, was named *Shantungosaurus* (shan tuhng uh SAWR uhs), or "Shantung lizard."

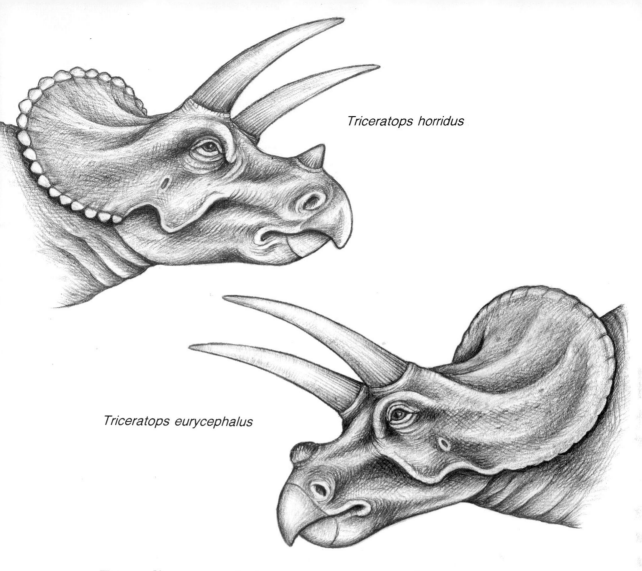

Triceratops horridus

Triceratops eurycephalus

Every dinosaur gets two names—a *genus* (JEE nuhs) name and a *species* (SPEE sheez) name. A genus name tells what kind of dinosaur it is, such as a *Triceratops* (try SEHR uh tahps), or "three-horned face." But there are often several kinds of just slightly different creatures in any genus group, and these are called species. So, each species gets a name that identifies it. Thus, the biggest kind of *Triceratops* is named *Triceratops horridus* (HAWR ihd uhs), or "dreadful

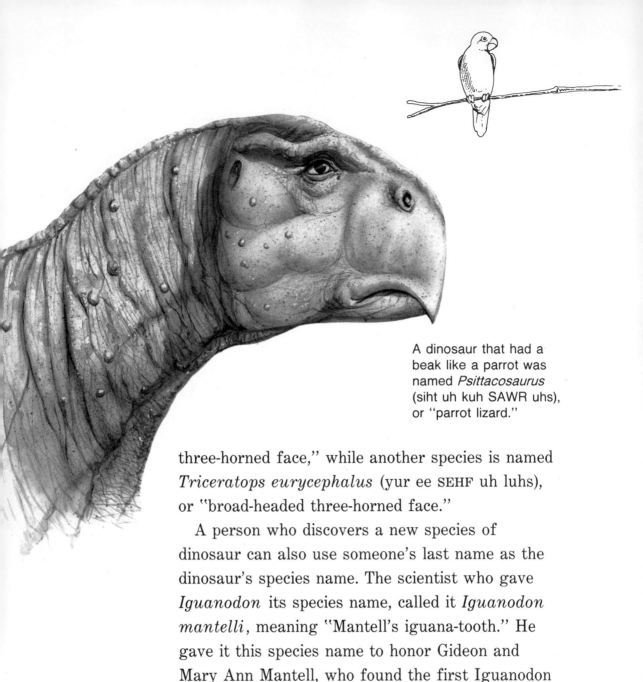

A dinosaur that had a beak like a parrot was named *Psittacosaurus* (siht uh kuh SAWR uhs), or "parrot lizard."

three-horned face," while another species is named *Triceratops eurycephalus* (yur ee SEHF uh luhs), or "broad-headed three-horned face."

A person who discovers a new species of dinosaur can also use someone's last name as the dinosaur's species name. The scientist who gave *Iguanodon* its species name, called it *Iguanodon mantelli*, meaning "Mantell's iguana-tooth." He gave it this species name to honor Gideon and Mary Ann Mantell, who found the first Iguanodon fossils. Last names have also been used as genus names for dinosaurs. One dinosaur is called Lambeosaurus (lam bee uh SAWR uhs), or "Lambe's lizard," after Lawrence Lambe, who helped discover several kinds of dinosaurs.

Dinosaur names can get changed, and many have. This usually happens because a person finds what they think is a new dinosaur and gives it a new name. Then it turns out to be a known dinosaur. When *Hylaeosaurus* was named, scientists weren't sure what kind of dinosaur it was. Some years later, an armored dinosaur was found and named *Polacanthus* (pahl uh KAN thuhs), or "many thorns." But, long afterwards, more *Hylaeosaurus* fossils were found, and it turned out that *Hylaeosaurus* and *Polacanthus* were the same. So the name *Polacanthus* was dropped. The older name, *Hylaeosaurus*, is now the official name for that kind of dinosaur.

Scientists gave this dinosaur the name *Struthiomimus* (stroo thee uh MY muhs), or "ostrich imitator," because it seemed much like an ostrich.

A dinosaur dictionary

Here is an alphabetical listing of all the dinosaurs presented in this book, with the pronunciation and meaning of each dinosaur's name. The page number tells you where you can find information about that dinosaur.

How do we know about dinosaurs?

All our knowledge of dinosaurs comes from the remains of some of these creatures—remains that were preserved by chance for many millions of years. This happened in any one of a number of different ways.

A dinosaur swimming in a lake one day might have suddenly died from disease, from old age, or even by accidentally drowning. Its body sank down into the mud at the bottom of the lake. As time went by, the dead dinosaur's flesh began to rot until only its skeleton was left.

Tiny specks of sand, soil, and volcanic ash, dropped by the wind or washed into the lake with rain water, constantly sank onto the mud at the lake bottom. Slowly, the dinosaur's bones were covered up.

As thousands and then millions of years went by, the mud grew deeper and deeper. The enormous weight of all the mud on top squeezed the mud at the bottom together until it became rock. The dinosaur skeleton was buried inside the rock.

Bones have many tiny hollow places in them. All this time, water was seeping into the hollow places in the dinosaur's bones. There were tiny bits of rock in the water, and this rock slowly filled all the

How dinosaurs became fossils

1.

2.

3.
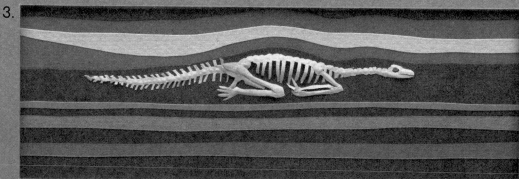

4.
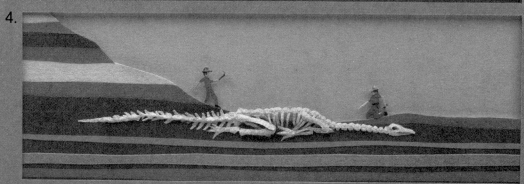

1. A dinosaur dies and sinks to lake bottom.
2. Flesh decays and bones are slowly covered by sand.
3. The sand becomes rock over millions of years.
4. The rock wears away, uncovering the fossil bones.

This dinosaur skeleton *(lower right)* was revealed when erosion wore away the rocky hillside.

hollow places. In time, the bones became part rock. This made them harder and helped preserve them.

Over millions of years, the lake dried up and disappeared. From time to time, earthquakes pushed up layers of rock that had been the lake's muddy bottom. For more millions of years, the rock was exposed to sun, wind, rain, snow, and sleet. Slowly, these forces wore away the rock until the dinosaur skeleton was finally revealed— waiting to be found. When scientists find a complete dinosaur skeleton, it's like finding treasure. It is from such preserved fossil skeletons that we have learned most of what we know about dinosaurs.

Another important kind of fossil was created in a different way. When some dinosaurs died, instead of their bodies being eaten or mostly rotting away, hot sunshine and dry weather dried them up. Their scaly skin was stretched tight over the bones. Mud or sand covered the dried bodies and, in time, they turned to stone, in the same way that dinosaur bones were fossilized. Thus, mummified dinosaur bodies with scaly skin on them were preserved.

Dinosaur eggs have been preserved, too. This happened if a sudden flash flood buried them or if they were buried by a sandstorm. Then the baby dinosaurs never hatched. In time, the eggs turned to stone.

But one important kind of fossil did not result from the death of a dinosaur, but by the actions of live ones. Dinosaurs that walked or trotted over muddy ground left footprints. Hot sun baked the mud dry, preserving the prints. Then, a dust storm or sandstorm covered the prints and protected them. Over a great amount of time, the dried mud turned into rock, preserving the footprints forever. In the same way, when a dinosaur let its tail rest on muddy ground for a moment, a print of its skin was made.

Bones, eggs, footprints, skin prints, and mummies—it is from remains such as these, preserved by chance for millions of years, that we have learned so much about dinosaurs.

What dinosaur bones
can tell us

A dinosaur skeleton can tell us a great deal about the original creature. It shows us exactly how big the animal was, of course, and gives us a good idea of what the animal looked like. Until some whole skeletons of *Iguanodon* were found, scientists thought iguanodons were four-footed creatures with horns on their noses. But the skeletons revealed that iguanodons often walked upright on two legs, and that the "horns" were actually big, spiky claws that were its thumbs.

At one time, it was thought that *Iguanodon* looked as shown in the old drawing on the opposite page. But when skeletons *(right)* were found, scientists saw that *Iguanodon* really looked like the model shown below.

From a whole skeleton, scientists can figure out how much a dinosaur weighed and how bulky it was when it was alive. Sometimes a whole skeleton can also provide some very special information, such as what the dinosaur ate. For example, some skeletons have been found with the bones of other creatures *inside* them, showing that the dinosaurs had eaten those creatures.

Even a single dinosaur bone or a dinosaur skull can provide much information. A thick, solid bone means that an animal was probably fairly slow-

These *Apatosaurus* tailbones have the teeth marks of an *Allosaurus* in them, which shows that allosauruses ate apatosauruses!

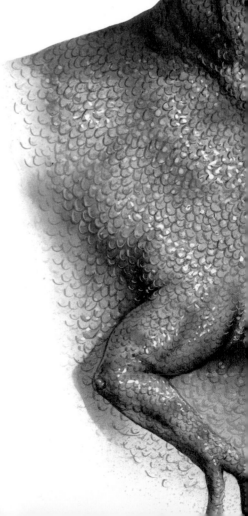

From the skull of a *Tyrannosaurus,* scientists made a cast of the brain. The brain *(right)* is shown in the same size scale as the head in the art above.

moving. A slim, hollow bone is from an animal that was surely a fast runner. A bone with teeth marks on it reveals that the dinosaur was food for another kind of dinosaur. Single bones have been found that show dinosaurs had certain kinds of diseases and that they suffered injuries. As for dinosaur skulls, by examining the inside of a skull, scientists can find out a lot about a dinosaur's brain, eyesight, and hearing.

We have gained much of our knowledge of dinosaurs from their bones!

What dinosaur teeth can tell us

The fossil teeth of a dinosaur show what kind of food it ate. And when scientists know what a dinosaur ate, that sometimes helps them figure out other things about it.

Sharks and some other meat-eating creatures of today have slightly curved, sharp-pointed teeth with jagged edges that are like the blade of a saw. These are teeth for cutting meat. Dinosaurs that had the same kind of teeth—such as tyrannosaurs (tih RAN uh sawrz) or megalosaurs (MEHG uh luh sawrz)—were obviously meat-eaters.

On the other hand, the teeth of some of the long-necked, long-tailed sauropods were like blunt pegs. Such teeth were probably used for raking in soft plants. The duckbilled dinosaurs and the horned dinosaurs had hard, twisty teeth that grew close together in many rows in the back of the mouth. These dinosaurs must have used the rows of teeth to grind up tough plant stems, making them soft enough to swallow.

The kind of dinosaurs known as ostrich imitators (because they looked like ostriches, but with a tail and arms instead of wings) did not have any teeth. Their jaws formed a beak, just like the beak of an ostrich. Because they looked so much like

The sharp teeth of a tyrannosaur show that it was a meat-eater.

Scientists can tell that the teeth in the skull of this duckbilled dinosaur were good for grinding up tough plants.

ostriches, scientists think they probably ate the same sort of things ostriches eat—fruits, plants, and small animals.

Knowing what a dinosaur ate helps scientists figure out other things about it, such as where it lived. A dinosaur that ate leaves almost surely lived in a forest, where there were plenty of leaves. A dinosaur that ate soft plants of the kind that generally grow near water probably lived in a swampy place.

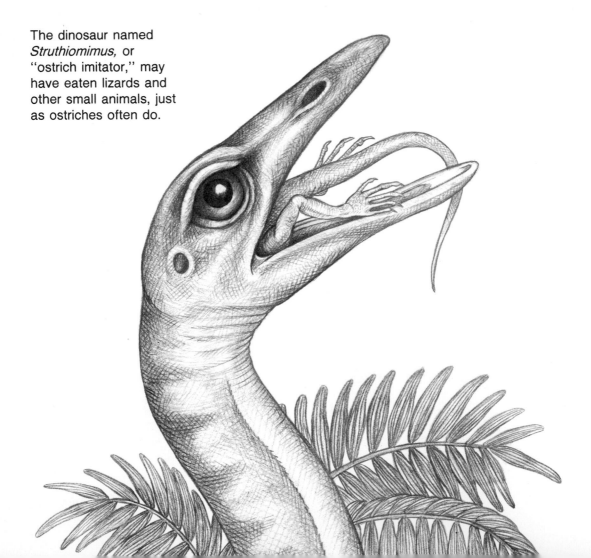

The dinosaur named *Struthiomimus,* or "ostrich imitator," may have eaten lizards and other small animals, just as ostriches often do.

These are the fossil footprints of a meat-eating carnosaur and a plant-eating sauropod. The meat-eater seems to have been tracking the big plant-eater!

What dinosaur footprints can tell us

Dinosaur footprints preserved in stone can provide a lot of information. By matching the bony fossil foot of a dinosaur to a footprint, scientists often can tell what kind of dinosaur made the footprints. And the footprints sometimes reveal exciting things about that kind of dinosaur.

For one thing, footprints can show the ways different kinds of dinosaurs moved. By measuring the distance between footprints and using some arithmetic, it is possible to figure out how fast some dinosaurs could walk or run. Some, such as the huge sauropods and big meat-eaters like *Tyrannosaurus* (tih ran uh SAWR uhs), or "tyrant lizard," walked quite slowly. But footprints of some of the smaller, lighter, two-legged dinosaurs show that they moved swiftly, running and leaping.

Footprints can also reveal how dinosaurs lived. A large number of sauropod footprints found in one place seem to show that these big dinosaurs were moving in a herd. The footprints in the middle are small, while those on the outside are large. Scientists think this means that the sauropods kept

their young ones in the middle, where they would be safe, and that the biggest sauropods were on the outside, as guards.

Footprints have been found in rock that was once the muddy bottom of a lake or stream. These prints show that big sauropods and big meat-eaters could swim. Among a series of *Iguanodon* footprints, there is a tail print. It shows that the dinosaur apparently got tired and sat down to rest for a while.

Some of the most exciting footprints ever found show the feet of a big meat-eater, probably an *Allosaurus* (al uh SAWR uhs), or "different lizard," following the footprints of a big plant-eating sauropod. It looks very much as if the *Allosaurus* was hunting the sauropod. Did it catch its prey?

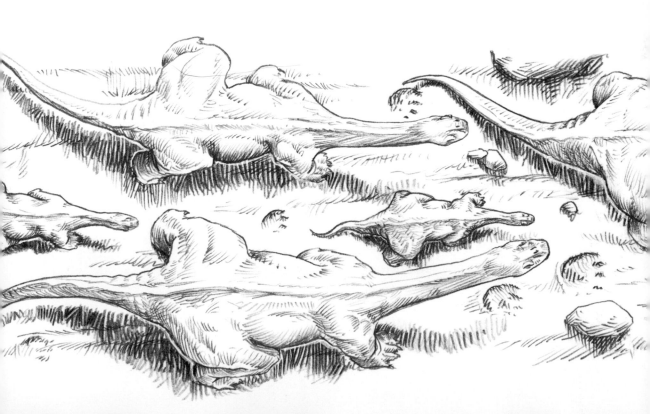

What dinosaur skin prints can tell us

The prints of dinosaur skin that scientists have found were made in several different ways. One kind of print was made by an animal's body lying in mud that later hardened into stone. Another kind was made when a dinosaur stopped for a moment and rested its tail on muddy ground. The very best kind is of dinosaurs that were mummified. After they died, the skin was

When this *Anatosaurus* died, its skin was preserved because it dried and turned to stone. Thus, we can see what the skin looked like when the animal was alive.

preserved when hot sunlight dried it out so that it shrank tightly over the bones. Later, both skin and bones were turned into rock.

All these prints show that dinosaurs had scaly skin, just as reptiles of today do. A skin print of one of the duckbilled dinosaurs shows skin like that of the lizard called a Gila (HEE luh) monster— thick and leathery and covered with little knobs

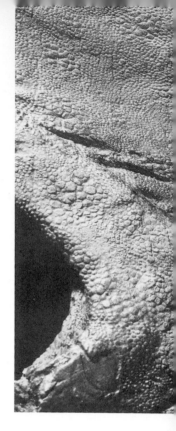

and bumps. Some of the bumps are larger than others and are arranged in little clusters. These clusters may have formed spots of color on the dinosaur's skin.

Because we know that dinosaur skin was like the skin of today's reptiles, it's a good guess that dinosaurs were probably colored a lot like today's reptiles, too. Like forest-dwelling lizards of today, dinosaurs that lived in forests may have been striped and splotched with greens and blacks that would help them blend into a background of green leaves and dark shadows. Those that lived in open, desertlike places may have been yellow or brown. Big sauropods, like the biggest land animals of today, elephants and rhinoceroses, were probably dark gray, or perhaps grayish-green.

This piece of fossilized *Anatosaurus* skin has clusters of knobs and bumps on it. These may have formed spots of color on the animal's body, as shown below.

What dinosaur eggs can tell us

Most reptiles of today have babies by laying eggs. Inasmuch as dinosaurs were reptiles, it isn't surprising that many kinds of them—perhaps all—laid eggs, too. A number of different kinds of fossil dinosaur eggs have been found. They were preserved for millions of years in much the same way that dinosaur bones sometimes were.

Mussaurus egg

Hypselosaurus egg

Protoceratops egg

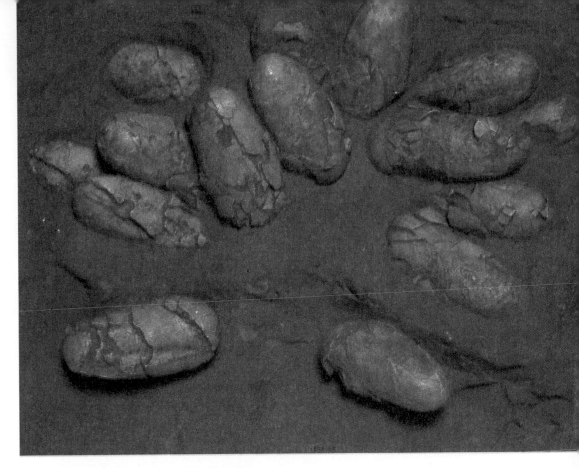

This nest of fossil eggs of the dinosaur
Protoceratops was discovered in Mongolia.

You might think the egg of an enormous
dinosaur would be huge, but this isn't the case.
The biggest dinosaur egg yet found is that of a
sauropod called *Hypselosaurus* (hihp sehl uh SAWR
uhs), or "high lizard." Hypselosaurus was 40 feet
(12 meters) long, but the egg is a round ball only
about 10 inches (25 centimeters) wide. Most other
dinosaur eggs are smaller. The smallest egg, that
of a dinosaur named *Mussaurus* (muh SAWR uhs),
or "mouse lizard," is only an inch (2.5 cm) long!

Many reptiles of today, such as sea turtles, simply lay their eggs, cover them with sand, and leave them to hatch in the warmth of the sun. They don't take care of their babies. Some dinosaurs probably did the same thing. But in other cases, the eggs and skeletons of baby dinosaurs seem to show that some kinds of dinosaurs took very good care of their young, in much the same way that most birds now do.

In Montana, a nest of a dinosaur named

Maiasaura (my uh SAWR uh) contained both
unhatched eggs and the skeletons of baby
dinosaurs of several different sizes. Scientists
think this means that the young dinosaurs stayed
in the nest until they were big enough to take care
of themselves. Until then, the parent dinosaurs
must have taken care of them, bringing them food
and guarding them from attackers. This is why
scientists gave these dinosaurs the name
Maiasaura, which means "good-mother lizard."

What the earth
can tell us about dinosaurs

The rock that forms the crust of the earth is in layers. These layers often look very different from one another because they were formed at different periods in the past. Scientists have ways of telling when each layer was formed. Thus, it is possible to tell how old dinosaur bones, or footprints, or eggs are from the layer of rock in which they are found. And, of course, this tells us when different kinds of dinosaurs lived.

Dinosaur fossils aren't the only things found in layers of ancient rock. There are also fossilized plants, seeds, and even pollen. These things, and even the kind of rock itself, can tell us a great deal about what the world was like when different kinds of dinosaurs were alive.

The first dinosaurs appeared about 230 million years ago, and the last died out around 65 million years ago. For 165 million years, dinosaurs were about as common as birds are today. During all those millions of years, many different kinds of dinosaurs appeared. The last kinds of dinosaurs were descendants of earlier kinds, but generally looked much different from their ancestors.

The long period of time during which the dinosaurs lived is called the Mesozoic (mehs uh ZOH

This mountain in New Mexico has all the layers of rock formed during the three periods of the Mesozoic Era. Different kinds of dinosaurs lived in each period. Their fossils are found in the rock layers formed during the period in which they lived.

ihk) Era. The Mesozoic Era is divided into three time periods—the Triassic (try AS ihk), Jurassic (ju RAS ihk), and Cretaceous (krih TAY shuhs). In each of these periods, different kinds of rock were formed and different kinds of dinosaurs existed.

Size comparisons

The boy and girl in this picture are about 4½ feet (1.3 meters) tall—the average size of a nine-year-old. To help you understand the size of the dinosaurs described in this book, you will find a picture of a child standing by an outline picture of each dinosaur. Both are drawn so that they are in the proper size to each other.

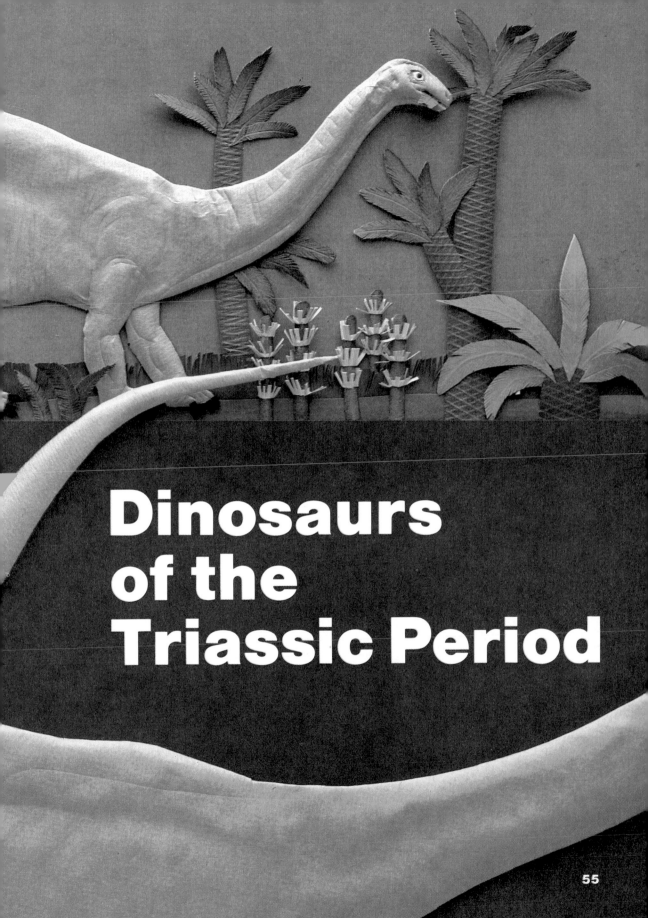

Dinosaurs
of the
Triassic Period

The coming
of the dinosaurs

During the time from 245 million to 208 million
years ago, three layers of reddish rock formed, one
on top of the other, on many parts of the earth.
Scientists call the 37-million-year period of time
during which this rock formed the Triassic (try AS
ihk) Period. *Triassic* means "three," referring to
the three layers of rock. During this period, the
first dinosaurs appeared.

At the beginning of the Triassic Period, the earth was very different from the way it is now. Today, there are seven continents spread out over the globe. But then, there was only one gigantic continent in the center of a vast ocean. The weather of this very different world was hot as summer all year long, and very dry. There was very little rain and never any snow, anywhere. There weren't even any great sheets of ice at the North and South poles as there are now.

Much of the huge continent was a dry, barren desert of sand and low hills of rock. But thick forests grew along the banks of rivers and spread out across the muddy deltas that formed where the rivers flowed into the ocean. Some of the trees in these forests were like some of the palm trees and fir trees of today, but others had short, ball-shaped trunks sprouting clusters of long, feathery leaves. Some were like the little horsetails, or scouring rushes, that grow beside ponds and streams today, but hundreds of times larger. There was no grass or flowers to sway in the wind.

Insects, spiders, and centipedes swarmed through these forests, but there were no butterflies or bees. Most of the creatures that crept and crawled and scurried among the plants were scaly skinned reptiles. Reptiles resembling crocodiles swam in the rivers, and bumpy-shelled turtles crawled along the muddy banks. Lizards and lizardlike creatures prowled in search of insects or reptiles smaller than themselves.

These were all four-legged animals. But in time, one kind of small, slim reptile became able to get up on its two back legs to chase after prey. These reptiles were the ancestors of the dinosaurs. As time went on, their descendants became more and

more numerous and spread out across the land.
Over millions of years, many kinds of dinosaurs
appeared.

   Toward the end of the Triassic Period, other new
creatures also appeared—winged, flying reptiles,
and little, furry, shrewlike animals that were the
first kinds of mammals. The first kinds of birds
also probably appeared during the Triassic Period.

Chindesaurus

(chihn duh SAWR uhs)

About 225 million years ago, a long-necked, long-tailed reptile plodded along on all four legs through a forest. It was a bulky beast, about 3 feet (1 meter) high at the hips and weighing a good 200 pounds (91 kilograms).

Coming to a narrow stream, the reptile waded across to the other side. Here, there grew some stubby trees, only about 6 feet (1.8 m) tall, with clusters of leaves at their tops. The reptile trudged over to one of the trees and stood up on its back legs. Now it was tall enough to reach the leaves.

This animal of 225 million years ago is the oldest dinosaur we know of—one of the first kinds. It lived in what is now a desert in the state of Arizona. Its name means "ghost lizard." It was given this name because its fossil bones were found at a place in the desert called Chinde Point. *Chinde* is an American Indian word for "ghost."

Staurikosaurus
(stawr ihk uh SAWR uhs)

Another kind of very early dinosaur, that was
quite different from *Chindesaurus*, lived in South
America about 220 million years ago. It was slim,
with a long, slender tail, a short neck, and rather
large head. It was about 6½ feet (2 meters) long,
but it weighed only about 70 pounds (32
kilograms). It was a fast runner that probably
chased after smaller creatures, for its sharp teeth
show that it was a meat-eater.

This animal has been named *Staurikosaurus*,

which means "cross lizard." The name refers to a
group of stars called the Southern Cross. This star
group forms a cross in the sky in the Southern
Hemisphere.

Staurikosaurus is the very first saurischian, or
lizard-hipped, dinosaur we know of. In some ways
it is like both of the two different kinds of
saurischian dinosaurs that were common millions
of years later—the big meat-eaters such as
Tyrannosaurus and the huge plant-eaters such as
Apatosaurus (ap uh tuh SAWR uhs). Perhaps some
of the descendants of *Staurikosaurus* were
ancestors of these two kinds of dinosaurs.

Herrerasaurus

(eh ray rah SAWR uhs)

Several million years after the time of *Staurikosaurus*, a bigger, heavier, meat-eating dinosaur lived in what is now the country of Argentina, in South America. It has been named *Herrerasaurus* ("Herrera lizard"), after the place where its fossil bones were found.

An *Herrerasaurus* was about 10 feet (3 meters) long and weighed some 220 pounds (100 kilograms). It had curved, sharp teeth in big jaws. Like *Staurikosaurus* it was a lizard-hipped dinosaur. Even though it was a meat-eater, some scientists think it may have been the direct ancestor of the big, lizard-hipped, plant-eating sauropod dinosaurs that lived much later.

Some dinosaurs very much like *Herrerasaurus*, only smaller, also lived in other parts of Argentina and in China.

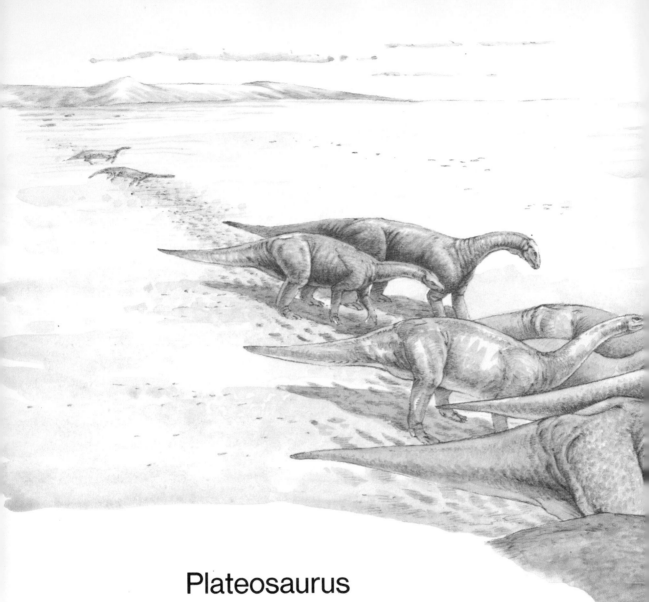

Plateosaurus
(plat ee uh SAWR uhs)

Some 215 million years ago, in what is now a part of Germany, a herd of dinosaurs came trudging out of a desert onto a bit of green land that formed the shore of a wide inland sea.

These dinosaurs—big, bulky reptiles with long necks and long tails—were nomads, who traveled

from one place to another during a year. They had been living in hilly country beyond the desert, but it was the dry season of the year now and food had grown scarce there. So they had crossed the desert, a journey of about 75 miles (121 kilometers) that had taken three days, to come to where food was still plentiful.

They had plodded across the desert on all four feet, which was the most comfortable way for such large, heavy animals to walk. But now, as they came in sight of stubby-trunked trees with circles of feathery leaves at the top, some of the reptiles stood up on their hind legs and trotted eagerly toward the nearest trees. Standing upright, they could easily reach the leaves at the top of the short trunks. Contentedly, they began to munch, their teeth easily cutting through tough leaves and stems.

However, many of the animals stayed on all fours. There were enough juicy plants on the ground to satisfy them. They, too, began to eat at once. It had been a hard, hungry trip across the barren desert. Indeed, some of the herd's youngest and weakest members had died on the way.

These dinosaurs, which have been named *Plateosaurus*, or "flat lizard," were the kind of dinosaurs known as prosauropods. They were much like the huge, bulky, four-legged sauropod dinosaurs that came later. But even though plateosauruses were fairly big and heavy—a full-grown one was about 20 feet (6 meters) long—they could walk on two legs at times. While their ancestors had been meat-eaters, plateosauruses were strictly plant-eaters.

Fossil bones and skeletons of dinosaurs very much like *Plateosaurus* have been found in North America, southern Africa, China, and Argentina, as well as Germany.

Riojasaurus

(ree oh hah SAWR us)

The biggest dinosaur we know of from the Triassic Period is a prosauropod, like *Plateosaurus*. It has been named *Riojasaurus* ("Rioja lizard") from the part of Argentina where it was found.

Riojasaurus was as much as 36 feet (11 meters) long. It was so bulky and heavy that it probably went on all fours all the time. Like *Plateosaurus* and most other prosauropods, its front feet had five "fingers," with a long, sharp, curved claw on each thumb. This hooked claw may have been used to dig and pull up plant roots or to pull leafy branches to the animal's mouth. Or, perhaps it was a weapon with which to jab and slash at an enemy.

Riojasaurus was very different from most prosauropods in one special way. Most prosauropods probably ate only plants, but *Riojasaurus* may have been a meat-eater. Its teeth were sharp and pointed, like the teeth of meat-eating dinosaurs. However, such a big, heavy creature as a *Riojasaurus* could never have chased after prey. If it did eat meat, it must have

eaten the bodies of dead creatures that it found as it walked about.

Scientists once thought that big prosauropods such as *Riojasaurus* were the ancestors of the gigantic sauropods like *Apatosaurus* and *Brachiosaurus* (brak ee uh SAWR uhs). They did look like them, but it is now known that the prosauropods were a separate family. Prosauropods lived for several million years after the end of the Triassic Period. Then they all died out.

skeleton of a baby *Mussaurus*

Mussaurus
(muh SAWR uhs)

The smallest dinosaur skeleton yet discovered is only 8 inches (20 centimeters) long. Because of its tiny size, this dinosaur was named *Mussaurus*, or "mouse lizard."

However, this tiny skeleton is actually the skeleton of a baby *Mussaurus*. From its bones, we can tell that this kind of dinosaur was a prosauropod—one of the long-necked, long-tailed plant-eaters, like *Plateosaurus*. All of these dinosaurs were rather large. Thus the baby *Mussaurus* could have grown up to be as much as 10 feet (3 meters) or even 20 feet (6 m) long.

The little *Mussaurus* skeleton was found along with several other baby *Mussaurus* skeletons and two eggs. The eggs were no bigger than cherries. It looks as if the baby dinosaurs and the eggs were in a nest that had been made by their mother. This seems to show that the babies must have stayed in the nest until they were big enough to take care of themselves. Most reptiles of today leave the nest as soon as they hatch. So a mother *Mussaurus* must have brought food to her babies and kept watch over them.

In the case of the baby *Mussaurus* skeletons, something must have happened. Perhaps the mother was killed, or maybe the nest was covered over by a mudslide. At any rate, the babies died and were fossilized.

Mussauruses lived in what is now Argentina, in South America.

Coelophysis
(see LOH fuh sihs)

A reddish-brown plain, dotted with pale green clumps of ferns, stretched away on all sides. In the distance, a slow-moving river wound across the plain. The trees and plants growing along the riverbank formed a long, shaggy line of dark green. Farther away rose the brown, massive cone of a volcano.

On one part of the plain a crowd of animals moved about. They looked and acted very much

like large, slim birds. They paced and trotted on
birdlike legs and feet, and their long jaws were
much like the long, pointed bill of a crane or heron.
They twisted their long necks, as a stork or swan
might do. But instead of wings, they had long
arms. Instead of feathers, they had scales. And
they had long, snaky tails. Rows of sharp little
teeth gleamed in their jaws.

They were reptiles—birdlike saurischian

(lizard-hipped) dinosaurs. The biggest stood about 3 feet (1 meter) tall, and from nose to tail was about 10 feet (3 m) long.

Near one of these dinosaurs, a little lizard, about a foot (30 centimeters) long, was suddenly startled from its hiding place under a rock. As it skittered away over the sandy red soil, the dinosaur instantly gave chase. With its body bent forward, its long neck and long tail stretched straight out, it

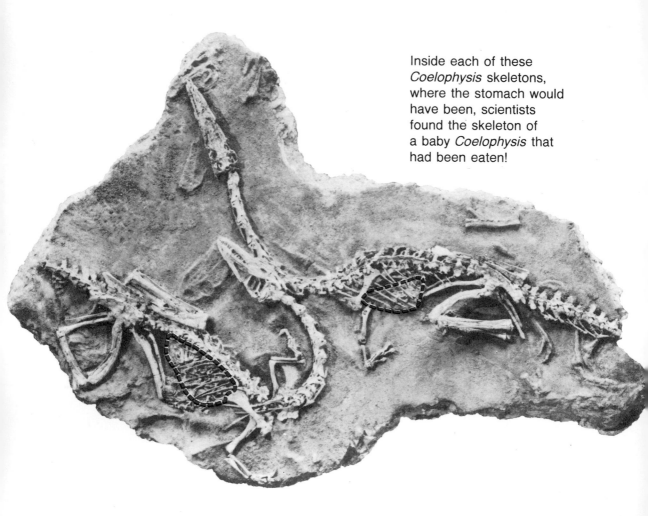

Inside each of these *Coelophysis* skeletons, where the stomach would have been, scientists found the skeleton of a baby *Coelophysis* that had been eaten!

raced after the lizard. Then it jabbed its head down and its pointed teeth pierced the lizard's body. It stopped running and straightened up. Holding the lizard in its clawed hands, the dinosaur gobbled it down in a few bites.

We call these slender, birdlike dinosaurs *Coelophysis*, meaning "hollow form." The name refers to the fact that, like birds, these dinosaurs had hollow bones. This means they were quick-moving. Their sharp teeth show they were meat-eaters, so they probably hunted by chasing any small creatures they could catch—large insects, lizards and other small reptiles, and little mouselike mammals. There is clear evidence that a hungry grown-up *Coelophysis* would also eat a baby *Coelophysis*. *Coelophysis* skeletons have been found with the bones of young coelophysises inside them, where the stomach would have been!

From the large number of skeletons and tracks that have been found together, it seems clear that these dinosaurs lived in packs, as wolves and hyenas do today. Perhaps they hunted in packs— teaming up to pull down and share some larger creature.

Coelophysis fossils have been found in several parts of the United States. And dinosaurs very much like *Coelophysis*, some larger and some smaller, also lived in what are now Scotland, Germany, and China.

Lesothosaurus

(luh soh toh SAWR uhs)

The broad, brown plain baked under a fiercely hot sun. No rain had fallen for many days, and the few scrubby plants that dotted the plain were dry and yellowed. It was the beginning of the hot, dry season.

Side by side, in the shade of a big boulder, two small reptiles dug holes in the sandy brown soil. They were slim creatures, with long tails and long back legs with four-toed feet. Their front legs were like arms, with little five-fingered hands. They had short necks and small, lizardlike heads. From nose to tail tip they were only a little more than 3 feet (1 meter) long.

After a time, each reptile seemed to feel that its hole was just about right. Each worked its way down into its hole until only the tip of its nose showed. Now they would go into a kind of deep sleep for the rest of the hot season.

This was not something these creatures thought about doing. They did it because certain built-in "messages" in their brains made them do it. It was a way of staying alive during a time when there was little or no food. When rain fell again, and the kinds of plants they ate began to sprout up once more, they would awaken.

These two little reptiles were dinosaurs of the
kind that has been named *Lesothosaurus*, or
"Lesotho lizard." They are named for the country
in Africa—Lesotho—where they were discovered.

Lesothosaurus was a different kind of dinosaur
from most others of the Triassic Period. It was not
a saurischian, or lizard-hipped dinosaur, but an
ornithischian, or bird-hipped dinosaur. Dinosaurs
like *Lesothosaurus* were probably the ancestors of
all the many different kinds of bird-hipped,
plant-eating dinosaurs that spread throughout the
world for millions of years after the Triassic
Period ended.

These little dinosaurs were probably very fast
runners. They defended themselves from the
attacks of meat-eating dinosaurs and other reptiles
by simply running away.

Heterodontosaurus
(heht uhr uh dahn tuh SAWR uhs)

By the end of the Triassic Period there were several different kinds of ornithischian, or bird-hipped, dinosaurs. All were descended from *Lesothosaurus* and other earlier ornithischians. Still quite small, they could defend themselves only by running swiftly away from danger. But in several other ways they had changed.

For one thing, some of these little ornithischians now had cheeks, which no other kind of dinosaur had and which no reptile has today. The cheeks enabled them to hold large amounts of food in the mouth. If they had to suddenly run away from where they were eating, they could take some food with them.

Because of the shape of their feet, these dinosaurs are called ornithopods, or "bird feet." Ornithopods were the only kind of ornithischian dinosaurs that walked on two legs. There were other ornithischians, but they were all four-footed.

One kind of these little ornithopod dinosaurs has been named *Heterodontosaurus*, meaning "different-toothed lizard." Both males and females had two different kinds of teeth. In the front of the mouth were little teeth for biting, and back inside the cheeks were teeth for chewing. And the male *Heterodontosaurus* also had a third kind of tooth—a curved, sharp fang on each side of the mouth, between the biting and chewing teeth.

A *Heterodontosaurus* used its front teeth to snip off plant leaves and stems. Then it used its cheek teeth to chew the plants so it could swallow them. But no one is sure how a male *Heterodontosaurus* used its fangs. Surely these little animals couldn't

have used their fangs in defense against enemies—
to bite meat-eaters! Perhaps they used them against
each other, to nip and bite other males in fights over
females or territory.

A *Heterodontosaurus* was about 4 feet (1.2
meters) long. These little dinosaurs lived in what is
now South Africa.

Other animals
of the Triassic Period

The first kinds of dinosaurs of the Triassic Period shared the world with a great many other kinds of animals, mostly reptiles. Some of these other animals were far bigger than most of the dinosaurs and probably preyed on them. Some needed the same sort of food as dinosaurs, and so there was a struggle to see which kind of animal would survive. In time, the dinosaurs won out. Many of the other kinds of reptiles slowly died out, until they became extinct.

Many of the animals in the world when the first dinosaurs appeared were actually "leftovers" from the period before the Triassic. They were not reptiles, but were amphibians, like a frog. They hatched out of soft eggs that floated in water, and spent most of their lives in swamps and streams, living mainly on fish. They probably waddled up onto land once in a while. One of these creatures, called *Mastodonsaurus* (mas tuh dahn SAWR us), looked like a pudgy, short-tailed alligator. It was about 13 feet (4 meters) long.

These giant amphibians were all gone by the end of the Triassic Period. But small amphibians, much like frogs of today, lived on. They were probably food for certain kinds of dinosaurs.

Mastodonsaurus was a giant amphibian of the Triassic Period. In the distance is a *Coelophysis,* a dinosaur.

Another "leftover" was a big-headed, tusked reptile with a stout body and thick legs. These plant-eaters spent most of their time wading in lakes and streams. They were about 3 feet (1 m) long, and lived much as hippopotamuses do now.

Lystrosaurus
(lihs truh SAWR uhs),
a mammallike reptile

Megazostrodon (mehg
uh ZAHS truh dahn),
a mammal

There were a number of different kinds of these reptiles. All were rather different from dinosaurs and other reptiles. They were built more like a mammal—a furry animal such as a bear or dog— than like a reptile. Some kinds may have had hair on their bodies.

These rather strange animals were related to the kind of reptile that was the ancestor of mammals. They lived alongside dinosaurs for millions of years, but most were gone before the end of the Triassic Period. In their place, there were small, furry, four-footed animals that looked a bit like long-nosed mice or rats. These were the first kind of mammal—ancestors of all the furry animals in the world today. They were becoming common by the end of the Triassic, and were probably prey for *Coelophysis* and other meat-eating dinosaurs.

From the middle to the end of the Triassic, reptiles called rhynchosaurs (RIHNG koh sawrz), or "beaked lizards," were common almost everywhere. These four-footed creatures had a mouth like a beak that could dig up and chop through tough plant roots. Some were as much as 6 feet (1.8 m) long, but others were much smaller. Plant-eating dinosaurs and rhynchosaurs probably often shared the same feeding grounds. And meat-eating dinosaurs almost certainly preyed on the rhynchosaurs. Most rhynchosaurs died out by the end of the Triassic Period.

Reptiles called thecodonts (THEE kuh dahnts), meaning "socket-tooth," were also common during most of the Triassic Period. Many thecodonts were large, bulky, four-legged animals that looked somewhat like crocodiles. Others were small, slim, two-legged runners. Creatures such as these were actually the ancestors of the dinosaurs, but they and dinosaurs lived side by side for millions of years.

thecodont

rhynchosaur

The seas of the world in the Triassic Period abounded with many kinds of swimming reptiles. There were lizardlike creatures 10 feet (3 m) long, with long necks and tails, and webbed feet. They are called nothosaurs (NAHTH uh sawrz), meaning "fake lizards." They ate fish, and probably lived much as seals do today.

nothosaur

placodont

ichthyosaur

Tanystropheus

There were also reptiles that looked almost exactly like the dolphins of today. They are known as ichthyosaurs (IHK thee uh sawrz), or "fish lizards."

A very strange sea reptile of the Triassic Period was a creature that has been named *Tanystropheus* (tan ih STROH fee uhs), meaning "long twisted neck." It was 20 feet (6 m) long from the top of its nose to the end of its tail, but its long skinny neck made up about half of that length! A *Tanystropheus* probably couldn't have held its neck up for any length of time. Most of the time it may have had its long neck stretched straight out, ready to seize fish in its sharp-toothed jaws.

Swimming in shallow water near shore were stout-bodied, armored reptiles called placodonts (PLAK uh dahnts), meaning "plate-toothed." Most of them were about 6 feet (1.8 m) long. Placodonts ate oysters, mussels, and similar shellfish. They scooped these off the sea bottom with their shovellike front teeth. Then they used teeth like thick plates, in the back of the mouth, to crack the shellfish open.

Some placodonts changed a great deal during the Triassic Period. So, by the end of the period, there were placodonts with shells, like turtles, and with toothless, beaked jaws. But no placodont, nothosaur, or the *Tanystropheus* survived past the end of the Triassic Period. The ichthyosaurs, however, did.

Lizards and turtles appeared in the Triassic Period and became common. Lizards were probably the main prey of small, meat-eating dinosaurs such as *Coelophysis*. The first kinds of crocodiles also appeared and were in most streams and rivers by the end of the period. The first kinds of pterosaurs (TEHR uh sawrz), or "winged lizards," were soaring in the skies.

Birds probably also appeared during the Triassic Period. A creature that lived about 225 million years ago and that looked like a long-tailed, crow-sized dinosaur with wings may have been one of the first kinds of birds. It has been named *Protoavis* (proh toh AH vihs), or "first bird."

Protoavis

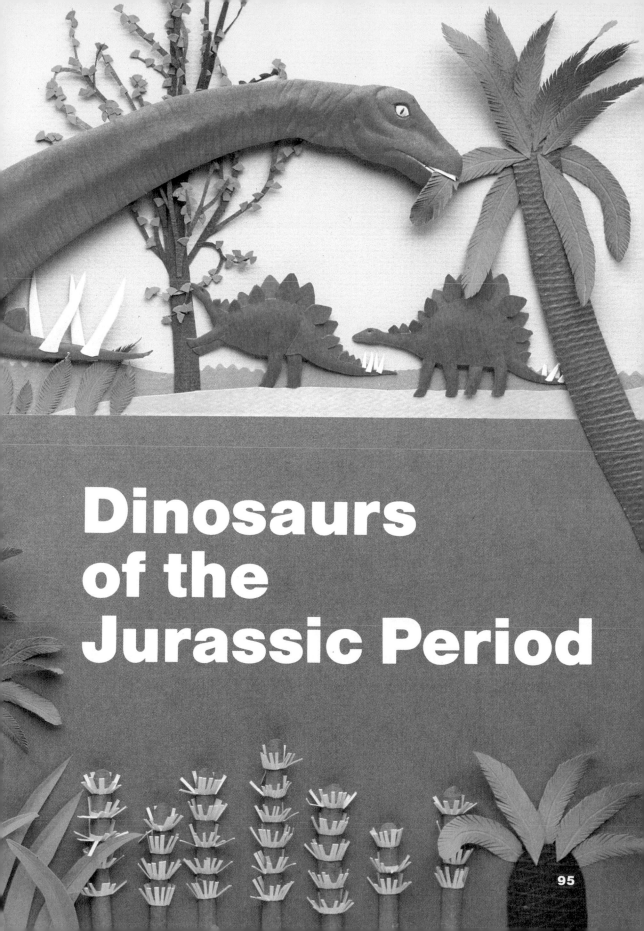

Dinosaurs of the Jurassic Period

The spreading
of the dinosaurs

From about 208 million to 144 million years ago—a total of 64 million years—many layers of rock formed on parts of the single huge continent that existed then. Most of these layers can be seen today in the Jura Mountains, in Europe. So, scientists call the period when these layers formed, the Jurassic, or "Jura rock," Period.

The weather during this period was still quite warm all year long. But the Jurassic Period was much wetter than the Triassic Period. Because of heavy rainfall, places that had been deserts during the Triassic Period became green with plants. In the lowlands, vast forests spread out and water collected to form great swamps. Trees similar to the evergreen trees and palm trees of today were common. But there were still no flowering plants or grass. And there were only a few of the kind of trees that shed their leaves each year.

Early in the Jurassic Period, the sea crept into many low parts of the great continent. Where there had been broad plains and wide valleys, there were now scattered islands and long fingers of land sticking out into the water. Plant life flourished in these places.

With so much vegetation there was an enormous food supply for plant-eating dinosaurs. They became more numerous and took on many new

The Jurassic Period gets its name from the Jura Mountains of Europe, in which the layers of rock formed during the period may clearly be seen.

forms. And, as the plant-eaters increased, so did
the meat-eaters. As certain kinds of plant-eating
dinosaurs got bigger and bigger, so did the
carnosaurs that preyed on them.

Frogs, of the sort there are now, appeared during the Jurassic Period. Birds and flying reptiles became more numerous, and so did the little furry, mouselike mammals.

Barapasaurus

(buh rap uh SAWR uhs)

It was during the Jurassic Period that the huge, long-necked, four-footed sauropod, or lizard-foot, dinosaurs became common. One of the first sauropods we know of lived at the beginning of the Jurassic Period, in what is now India. It has been named *Barapasaurus*, which means "big-leg lizard."

Barapasaurus was about 60 feet (18 meters) in length, with rather long, slim legs. Its teeth were somewhat spoon-shaped, with saw-toothed edges— very good for cutting through tough plant stems and leaves.

In some ways, a *Barapasaurus* looked like some of the big prosauropod dinosaurs such as *Riojasaurus*. But they were really not much alike. The front legs of prosauropods were like arms, with hands that had five separate fingers. But the front legs of most sauropods had wide, flat feet, like the feet of an elephant. Prosauropods had their nostrils at the end of a snout, as most animals do, but most sauropods had their nostrils up on the top of their heads. Prosauropods had teeth that were a lot like the teeth of meat-eating dinosaurs—sauropod teeth were the teeth of plant-eaters.

A number of kinds of prosauropods lived on past the Triassic Period, well into the Jurassic. But they all died out after a few million years. They just couldn't do as well as the sauropods.

Scutellosaurus
(skyoo tehl uh SAWR uhs)

Scutellosauruses lived about the beginning of the Jurassic Period, in what is now the state of Arizona. They were small dinosaurs, only about 4 feet (1.2 meters) long. More than half that length was made up of a long, long tail. They were plant-eaters, with little flattened pear-shaped teeth. The teeth had tiny jagged edges for cutting through tough plant stems and leaves.

The name *Scutellosaurus* means "small-shield lizard." This dinosaur was given that name because hundreds of little bony shields, called plates, covered its back and sides. These square-shaped plates had a ridge running down the middle that made them look like the roofs of tiny houses. It also seems that a row of bony triangles ran down a *Scutellosaurus*'s back and tail.

This armor may have been useful for keeping other creatures from biting into a *Scutellosaurus*, but it must have been rather heavy for such a little creature. *Scutellosaurus* was built like a two-legged dinosaur—the kind that walked on its back legs and used its front legs like arms. But *Scutellosaurus* had rather long and heavy front legs. This seems to show that because of the weight of its armor, *Scutellosaurus* may have often walked on all fours. Its extra-long tail may

have helped it keep its balance when it went on two legs.

Scutellosaurus is one of the first armored dinosaurs we know of. Some scientists think it may have been the ancestor of some of the armored dinosaurs that lived much later.

Dilophosaurus
(dy loh foh SAWR uhs)

At about the same time *Scutellosaurus* lived, and
in the same place, there was a big meat-eating
dinosaur that is a bit of a mystery. It is known as
Dilophosaurus, meaning "two-crested lizard." It
gets its name from two ridges, or crests, of very
thin bone, that ran side by side on its head, from
behind the eyes to the tip of the nose.

But the bone in those crests is as thin as paper.

And that is the mystery. What could such frail crests have been for? Some scientists think they might have been a sort of cooling device for keeping the dinosaur's head from getting too hot. Others think the crests were just a decoration, like the comb on a rooster's head, that perhaps only the male *Dilophosaurus* had. But no one is sure.

Dilophosaurus was 20 feet (6 meters) long. It had sharp teeth, and its three-fingered hands had sharp claws. From the look of its skeleton, it could have been a fierce hunter. But could it have attacked and fought other large dinosaurs without damaging its delicate crests? Did it prey only on small creatures such as *Scutellosaurus*? Or did it, perhaps, eat only the bodies of dead creatures that it found, as hyenas, vultures, and some other animals do now?

Scelidosaurus
(sehl uh duh SAWR uhs)

Scelidosaurus, or "limb lizard," lived in the early part of the Jurassic Period. It was about 11½ feet (3.5 meters) long—as long as a large automobile. It had a bulky body, thick legs, and a rather small head on a long neck. A *Scelidosaurus* probably moved about with its head close to the

ground. Its long neck would enable it to reach down and take bites off low-growing plants without having to crouch to get at them.

A *Scelidosaurus* was too slow-moving to be able to run away from hungry carnosaurs, but it was protected by armor. Rows of hard, bony points ran down the back and sides of its neck, body, and tail. It would probably have been very difficult for even a large carnosaur to bite into such a tough, spiky

mouthful. Many scientists think that scelidosauruses may have been the ancestors of the ankylosaurs, a group of armored dinosaurs that lived later.

Scelidosaurus fossils have been found as far apart as England and Tibet, in Asia. It is possible that these animals lived on all parts of the single, huge continent that made up all the land in the world at the beginning of the Jurassic Period.

Cetiosaurus

(see tee uh SAWR uhs)

Cetiosauruses were big, plant-eating
sauropod dinosaurs. They lived from
the middle of the Jurassic Period,
about 170 million years ago, to the
end of the period, 140 million years
ago. They had flat, spoon-shaped
teeth, good for biting off leaves.
These dinosaurs were from 45 to 60
feet (14–18 meters) long. Even a small
Cetiosaurus might weigh as much as
two or three Asian elephants!

Cetiosauruses were the first sauropod
dinosaurs to be discovered, but no one
knew it. In 1809, when *Cetiosaurus*
bones were first found, people didn't
know there ever had been such a thing
as a dinosaur. They thought such huge
bones must have come from a whale.

Twenty years later, a scientist decided the bones had actually come from an immense reptile that had certainly been as big as many whales. So, he gave it a name that means "whale lizard." However, he thought it had been a kind of gigantic crocodile. It wasn't until after other sauropod fossils had been found that scientists realized *Cetiosaurus* also had been one of those long-necked, long-tailed dinosaurs.

Cetiosauruses lived in what is now England, western Europe, and North Africa. Sauropods very much like them lived in Australia, the United States, China, and Argentina.

Stegosaurus
(stehg uh SAWR uhs)

Stegosauruses were large, plant-eating dinosaurs that lived for millions of years during the second half of the Jurassic Period. A *Stegosaurus* was about 30 feet (9 meters) long, with a heavy, bulky body. Its back legs were about 11 feet (3.4 m) long, but its front legs were only about 4 feet (1.2 m) long. Although its hips were up high, it could have stretched its head down to the ground. For such a big animal it had a very small head—only 16 inches (41 centimeters) long. Its brain was no bigger than a walnut!

Along its back and tail, a *Stegosaurus* had seventeen thin, flat pieces of bone covered with skin. These were shaped somewhat like roundish triangles, or like the top part of the spade symbol in a deck of cards. It is these bony triangles, which scientists call plates, that give *Stegosaurus* its name. These plates look very much like the old-fashioned tiles that at one time covered the roofs of many buildings, and *Stegosaurus* means "roofed lizard."

Those plates on a *Stegosaurus*'s back have been a puzzle to scientists for more than a hundred years. They weren't attached to the animal's skeleton, and so they were always found loose among the bones of every *Stegosaurus* skeleton that was discovered. Because of this, scientists were never quite sure just how they had been arranged on a *Stegosaurus*'s back.

The first scientist who found a *Stegosaurus* skeleton thought the plates had been in a single row. Later, others thought they must have been in two rows. However, if the plates were in two rows, no one was quite sure whether they were in pairs, side by side, or whether one row was slightly behind the other, making the plates "stepped," like footprints. But just a short time ago, it was found that the first scientist may have been right after all, that the plates were in a single row.

Another mystery is what the bony plates were for. Most scientists believe they were probably devices for helping a *Stegosaurus* warm up quickly if it had to. If a reptile is too cold, it becomes stiff and can't move well until it warms up. A cold *Stegosaurus* could have stood so that the broad, flat sides of the plates faced directly into the sun, to soak up lots of warm sunlight. Big blood vessels under the skin that covered the

Standing with the broad sides of its back plates facing the sun may have helped a *Stegosaurus* warm up. Standing with the thin edges of the plates facing the sun may have helped it cool off.

plates would have steadily carried the warmth down into the animal's body, quickly warming it up.

This would have also worked the opposite way. A reptile's body easily stores up heat. If too much heat is stored up, the reptile will die. If a *Stegosaurus* became too hot, it could have stood

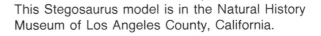

This Stegosaurus model is in the Natural History Museum of Los Angeles County, California.

for a while with only the thin edges of its plates facing into the sun, so they couldn't soak up any heat. This would have allowed heat to leak out of them into the air, making the *Stegosaurus* cooler.

Scientists agree that's how the plates could have worked if stegosauruses were "cold-blooded," as all reptiles are today. But some scientists don't think they were cold-blooded. So, they think the bony plates may have served to make a

Stegosaurus look bigger or to keep carnosaurs from jumping onto its back! Perhaps a *Stegosaurus* could move its back muscles so that the plates would point straight up or off to the side, depending upon where the carnosaur was trying to attack from. They might have looked dangerous enough to keep a carnosaur from jumping on them.

So, scientists don't agree about what a *Stegosaurus*'s back plates were for. But there's certainly no doubt about what a *Stegosaurus* used its tail for. It was a war club!

Four sharp, bony spikes, each about 3 feet (1 m) long, stuck up from the end of a *Stegosaurus*'s long, heavy tail. If a *Stegosaurus* swung its tail hard, slamming the spikes into the body of another

dinosaur, the spikes would have caused terrible wounds! We can imagine a *Stegosaurus* defending itself against a carnosaur by flailing away with its tail until the carnosaur, slashed and bleeding, finally limps away!

The front of a *Stegosaurus*'s mouth was a kind of beak, with sharp edges for snipping off the tops of low-growing plants. The teeth farther back in the jaws were rather weak, and could probably chew only very soft, juicy plants. Like most other ornithischian (bird-hipped) dinosaurs, *Stegosaurus* had cheeks, and could cram its mouth full of food.

Stegosauruses may have roamed about on the edges of lakes and swamps, feeding on the kinds of plants that grew thickly in such places. Some scientists think a *Stegosaurus* could have stood up on its back legs to reach plants in high places. Others think the animal was probably too heavy and bulky to do that.

Stegosauruses lived in what is now the western United States. Several kinds of slightly different stegosaurs have been found in other parts of the world.

Apatosaurus
(ap uh toh SAWR uhs)

Apatosaurus was one of the gigantic plant-eating sauropod dinosaurs. It was 70 feet (21 meters) long from the tip of its snout to the end of its tail. Its front legs were more than twice as tall as a tall man. It weighed 33 tons (30 metric tons), or more than five big African elephants.

The name *Apatosaurus* means something like "untrue lizard." Perhaps the scientists who named it could hardly believe such a gigantic animal was real. *Apatosaurus* is better known as *Brontosaurus* (brahn tuh SAWR uhs). The name means "thunder lizard," because an animal this size must have made a sound like the rumble of thunder when it walked.

The reason for the two names is because of a mix-up. When the animal was first discovered, it was named *Apatosaurus*. Later, a seemingly different animal was found and named *Brontosaurus*. Then, scientists realized that these two dinosaurs were the same. So, following

scientific rules, the first name used became the official name. But most people seem to like the second name better.

For a long time, most scientists thought that such huge, heavy creatures as apatosauruses would have had a hard time walking on land. It would have been much easier for them to stay in water, which could support their great weight. Scientists also believed *Apatosaurus*'s teeth were too weak to chew such things as tree leaves. If so, it could probably eat only the kinds of soft plants that grew in and around water. So it seemed as if apatosauruses must have spent most of their time wading and swimming in swamps or lakes, stretching their long necks to reach juicy plants growing at the water's edge.

Still another reason why scientists thought these animals must have been water dwellers was because of where their nostrils were. They didn't have nostrils at the end of the nose, as most land

animals do. Their nostrils were far up near the top of the head. It was thought that the animals must have been able to stand in very deep water with only the top of the head sticking out. It seemed as if this might have been a good way to hide from carnosaurs.

There seems to be some good evidence that sauropods such as *Apatosaurus* were, indeed, water-dwelling animals. We have found fossil footprints made by sauropods as they trudged through the shallow water of a muddy swamp. Another set of fossil footprints was made by a sauropod that was swimming in deep water. Its front feet left prints as the animal pushed itself along the bottom. Its back legs and tail must have been floating.

However, many scientists now think that *Apatosaurus* and other sauropods were not water creatures. They think these animals plodded about on dry land most of the time, in herds, like elephants. The scientists think that sauropods used their long necks to reach leaves at the top of tall trees. New information about the teeth of *Apatosaurus* shows that they weren't weak, and would have been very good for snipping leaves off trees.

There seems to be just as much evidence that sauropods were land animals as there is that they were water animals. For one thing, studies of the footprints of sauropods and the feet of sauropods such as *Apatosaurus* show that their feet were just like the feet of elephants—formed to hold the weight of a big, heavy animal as it walks about on the ground. And we have found fossil footprints made by a herd of sauropods as they marched along on solid ground.

Some scientists even think that the position of sauropod nostrils shows that these animals were more likely to have been land dwellers rather than water dwellers. For, water animals of today, such as crocodiles, hippopotamuses, and otters, do not have nostrils on top of the head, as sauropods did. Their nostrils are at the front. But there are some land animals that do have nostrils high on the head —elephants and tapirs, both of which have trunks. So, some scientists think that sauropods may have had some kind of trunk that helped them reach even higher!

If sauropods such as *Apatosaurus* were land animals, they were very slow-moving ones.

Some scientists think that *Apatosaurus* and other
sauropods may have had short trunks, like the tapirs
of today. This would have made it even easier for
them to reach the leaves of very tall trees.

Measurements of their fossil footprints show that
they couldn't have moved much faster than two to
four miles (3–6 kilometers) an hour, which is quite
slow. They certainly couldn't have run away from
a carnosaur such as *Allosaurus* or *Ceratosaurus*.
How could they have survived the attacks of
hungry meat-eaters?

Scientists think that *Apatosaurus* was well able
to defend itself. For one thing, *Apatosaurus* had a
long, powerful tail. If it used that tail like a whip,
it could have broken a carnosaur's bones and
injured it badly. Apatosauruses were also
much bigger than any carnosaur. If an
Apatosaurus reared up on its back legs and then

let itself fall forward onto a carnosaur, it could probably have crushed the smaller animal. This is how elephants sometimes defend themselves against tigers.

So, there seems to be a lot of evidence that sauropods such as *Apatosaurus* could have lived on land or in water. Perhaps they did both. They may have plodded about in the forests near swamps and streams, searching for food. Then, during the hottest part of the day, they might have gone into water to keep cool.

Apatosauruses lived in North America, in what are now the states of Colorado, Utah, Wyoming, and Oklahoma.

This *Apatosaurus* skeleton is at the Field Museum of Natural History in Chicago, Illinois.

An *Apatosaurus* might have defended itself by rearing up and then stomping on an attacking meat-eater.

Allosaurus
(al uh SAWR uhs)

During the Jurassic Period some kinds of meat-eating carnosaurs got bigger and bigger. One of the biggest was *Allosaurus*, a name that means "different lizard." An average-sized *Allosaurus* was about 36 feet (11 meters) long—longer than most buses. These were powerfully built animals that weighed as much as 4,000 pounds (1,800 kilograms). They had powerful legs and strong arms with sharp-clawed, three-fingered hands.

Many scientists think that *Allosaurus* was the tiger of its world—a fast-moving, ferocious hunter that could easily kill almost any animal. It might have prowled about until it sighted its prey, then

charged swiftly, running with its tail stretched
straight out and its head stretched forward. It
could have grasped its prey with its clawed hands
while it bit and ripped with the sharp teeth in its
huge jaws.

An *Allosaurus* fed by gulping down big pieces
of flesh that it tore off the bodies of dead
dinosaurs. Its giant jaws could take a very big
bite, and the bones of its skull could actually come
apart slightly, so that it was able to swallow
enormous chunks of meat.

We know for sure that allosauruses fed on some
of the biggest of all dinosaurs, the gigantic

sauropods such as *Apatosaurus*, which was 70 feet (21 m) long. We know this because the fossil bones of an *Apatosaurus*'s tail have been found with *Allosaurus* teeth marks on them and a couple of broken *Allosaurus* teeth mixed in with them. Obviously, a very hungry *Allosaurus*—so hungry that it broke some of its teeth while savagely biting into a bone—once feasted upon the flesh that covered the tail of an *Apatosaurus*.

But, had the *Allosaurus* actually killed the *Apatosaurus*, or was it simply feasting on part of a dead carcass it had found? Some scientists think allosauruses were not hunters, as lions and tigers are, but were more like a hyena or vulture, and ate dead animals they found—animals that had died in an accident or of old age.

However, there seems to be some evidence that allosauruses were hunters. Fossil footprints of a big sauropod dinosaur have been found with

This *Allosaurus* skeleton can be seen at the American Museum of Natural History in New York City.

footprints of an *Allosaurus* following after them. It certainly looks as if the *Allosaurus* was trailing the sauropod, because when the sauropod's footprints turn off in a different direction, the *Allosaurus* footprints turn after them. Was the *Allosaurus* keeping the big sauropod in sight, waiting for a chance to rush at it and leap on its back?

For millions of years, allosauruses lived in what is now North America, Africa, and China. Carnosaurs very much like them lived in all parts of the world.

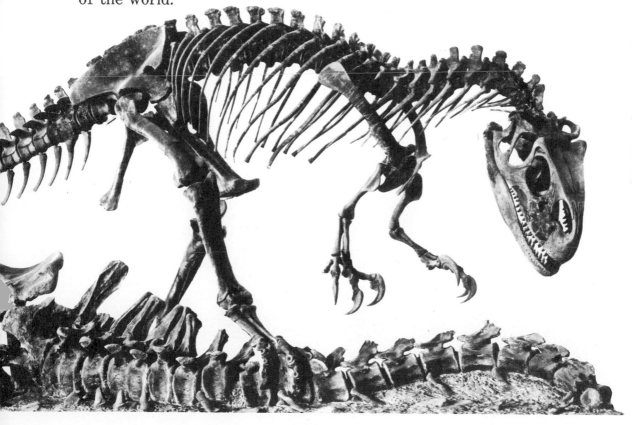

Kentrosaurus
(kehn truh SAWR uhs)

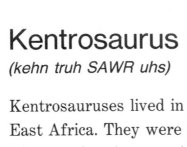

Kentrosauruses lived in what is now Tanzania in East Africa. They were four-legged plant-eaters, about 17 feet (5 meters) long.

These dinosaurs were closely related to the dinosaur called *Stegosaurus*. However, *Stegosaurus* had a row of spade-shaped bony plates along its back and tail. *Kentrosaurus* had plates on its neck and shoulders, and six pairs of long, pointed, bony spikes on its back and tail. But in most other ways, it was like a *Stegosaurus*.

If *Stegosaurus*'s bony plates were devices for helping it keep warm or cool, as many scientists

think, then perhaps that's what *Kentrosaurus*'s plates were for, too. But its sharp spikes look as if they were for protection, to keep carnosaurs from leaping on its back. *Kentrosaurus* even had a big, sharp spike sticking out of the upper part of each back leg, just below the hips. If a *Kentrosaurus* was threatened by a carnosaur, it probably turned its spiky back to its enemy and began waving its tail, which had two big, dangerous spikes at the end.

It is from all those spikes that *Kentrosaurus* gets its name, which means "pointed lizard." Scientists think these animals may have lived in herds, plodding about from place to place in search of low-growing, juicy plants.

Diplodocus
(duh PLAHD uh kuhs)

Diplodocus was one of the longest dinosaurs—as much as 88 feet (27 meters) long, from nose to tail. But it was rather slim and light compared to its close relative the *Apatosaurus*. Even though a *Diplodocus* was longer than an *Apatosaurus*, it weighed only some 11 tons (10 metric tons). *Apatosaurus* weighed three times as much.

Like other sauropod dinosaurs, *Diplodocus*'s way of life is a mystery. Was it a water-dwelling animal or a land-dwelling one? Its teeth could have been used for raking soft water plants out of a lake or swamp—but they could also have been used for combing leaves off tree branches. And the way the teeth are worn down in the jaws of some *Diplodocus* skulls seems to show that this is how they were used.

The bones in the tail of a *Diplodocus* also seem to show that it might have been a land animal. Toward the end of the tail, each bone has two little projections on the underside. One points forward and one backward. These projecting parts of the bone would have protected blood vessels from injury if the tail rubbed on the ground. So, some scientists think this means that a *Diplodocus* could have stood up on its back legs, with its tail pressed against the ground for support, and stretched its neck up to reach high growing leaves on tall trees.

These little projections, or beams, on the tail bones give *Diplodocus* its name, which means "double beam." Some tail bones of one *Diplodocus* also show that this *Diplodocus* had a disease called arthritis. This disease causes the cartilage covering the ends of bones to wear away, causing pain and swelling. Many people suffer from arthritis, so it wasn't just a dinosaur disease.

Camptosaurus
(kamp tuh SAWR uhs)

Camptosauruses were small, plant-eating ornithopods, or bird-footed dinosaurs, that were from 4 to 23 feet (1.2–7 meters) long. They lived in what is now the western part of North America and western Europe toward the end of the Jurassic Period. The name *Camptosaurus* means "bent lizard."

The front part of a *Camptosaurus*'s mouth was a toothless beak, like a bird's beak. But farther back, its upper and lower jaws were packed with bumpy teeth. Scientists think camptosauruses had a long, snaky tongue that they could wrap around branches or bunches of leaves. The tongue would pull the leaves into the mouth, the beak would snip them off the branch, and the teeth would grind them up for swallowing.

Camptosauruses may have lived in large herds out on open plains. They probably went on two legs most of the time, but could also have walked comfortably on all fours. They were rather heavily built and probably couldn't run very fast. So, living in herds on the open plains would have helped them survive. They would have been able to see carnosaurs approaching and would have had a head start running away. Only the oldest and slowest were likely to get caught.

Camarasaurus
(kam uh ruh SAWR uhs)

Camarasaurus was a sauropod dinosaur that was rather different from other sauropods such as *Apatosaurus* or *Diplodocus*. It had a shorter tail and neck and a much more blunt head. Its back sloped down toward the hips instead of upward. Instead of having a cluster of teeth like thin rods sticking out of the front of its mouth, it had rows of big, pointy teeth running around both jaws.

Camarasauruses were as much as 60 feet (18 meters) long and weighed as much as 20 tons (18 metric tons). But scientists were lucky enough to find the skeleton of a very young *Camarasaurus* that was only 16 feet (5 m) long. This skeleton shows the differences between a young dinosaur and a full-grown one. For its size, the young *Camarasaurus* had a larger head and shorter neck than a grown one.

Like other sauropods, Camarasaurus's nostril openings were on top of its head. So it, too, might have been either a water dweller or a land animal with a trunk.

Camarasaurus means "chambered lizard." This name was given to these sauropods because they had open places, like little chambers, or rooms, in their backbones. Camarasauruses lived in what is now the western United States.

Ceratosaurus
(sehr uh tuh SAWR uhs)

A large herd of camptosauruses browsed among clusters of giant ferns growing thickly around the edge of a lake. Most of the reptiles stood on all fours, but from time to time, one would rise up to look around, its jaws moving steadily as it chewed.

But the "lookouts" were caught by surprise. Five fierce dinosaurs suddenly rushed through the ferns at the camptosauruses. These animals were slightly smaller than the biggest of the camptosauruses, but the camptosauruses immediately fled in all directions. These attackers were deadly dangerous! Their sharp claws as well as the sharp teeth in their wickedly grinning jaws showed them to be meat-eaters. Some of them had a short, stubby horn on their nose.

Two of the frightened camptosauruses were a little slower than the rest. A pair of the quick-moving carnosaurs was on them at once. Using teeth and claws, they quickly killed the two camptosauruses. Shortly, all five carnosaurs were eating. Three of them clustered around one of the dead plant-eaters and two around the other.

A short time passed. Suddenly, the five carnosaurs lifted their heads. All turned to stare in the same direction. A new creature had stalked into view—an *Allosaurus*!

The *Allosaurus* plodded toward one half-eaten *Camptosaurus*. At once, the two horned

carnosaurs that had been feeding on the body backed away. The *Allosaurus* was nearly twice as big as they were, and they did not want to challenge it. The *Allosaurus* crouched down and began to eat.

An event such as that might have taken place about 140 million years ago in what is now the southwestern United States. All these dinosaurs lived there at that time. The small carnosaurs were the dinosaurs that have been named *Ceratosaurus*, meaning "horned lizard." A *Ceratosaurus* was from 15 to 20 feet (4.6–6 meters) long. Fossil footprints seem to show that these carnosaurs hunted and traveled in small packs as wolves and lions do today.

A *Ceratosaurus* wouldn't have used its horn to kill prey. It would have used its sharp claws and teeth for that. But then, what was the horn for?

Most scientists think that only the male ceratosauruses had a horn, and that they used this horn as male goats and deer use their horns and antlers when fighting each other at mating time. Had ceratosauruses fought with teeth and claws, one might have injured or even killed the other. But the short, stubby horn could not have done much harm. Two male ceratosauruses probably would have just poked and prodded each other and bumped their heads together. Finally one would give up and go away, leaving the winning male with a female. This is what many kinds of animals do at mating time.

In addition to the horn, ceratosauruses had a row of bony, skin-covered points running down the back and tail. Fossil *Ceratosaurus* bones have been found in East Africa as well as in North America.

Brachiosaurus
(brak ee uh SAWR uhs)

Brachiosauruses were among the biggest of all dinosaurs. A *Brachiosaurus* was from 75 to 90 feet (23–27 meters) long. Its head could be as much as 40 feet (12 m) above the ground—high enough to peer over the top of a four-story building! Such a creature weighed from 85 to 112 tons (77–102 metric tons). That is more than the total weight of fourteen of the biggest kind of elephants!

A *Brachiosaurus* was built much like a giraffe. That is, its front legs were longer than its back legs so that its back slanted down. It is because of the longer front legs (or upper "arms") that *Brachiosaurus* gets its name, which means "upper-arm lizard."

Some scientists think that brachiosauruses not only looked like giraffes but also lived much as giraffes do. They may have moved about the land in small herds, stretching their long necks up to browse on leaves at the very tops of the trees. They may have had trunks, to help them reach even higher.

This fossil skeleton of a *Brachiosaurus* is in a museum in East Germany. The human skeleton in front of the *Brachiosaurus* shows how truly gigantic the animal was.

Ultrasaurus

Brachiosaurus

However, other scientists think these huge, heavy creatures were more likely to have spent most of their time wading in the water of swamps or lakes. They might have fed on water plants or stretched their necks to feed on plants growing along the shore. They might have come onto land only for special reasons, such as to lay eggs.

Brachiosauruses belonged to a family of huge sauropod dinosaurs, all much alike, that we call brachiosaurids. Some of these brachiosaurids were apparently the biggest animals that have ever lived on land. A few bones of one of these creatures are so gigantic that scientists think the animal must have been more than 100 feet (30 m) long and weighed up to 150 tons (136 metric tons)—about as much as twenty big elephants! This dinosaur has been named *Ultrasaurus* (uhl truh SAWR uhs), which means something like "greatest possible lizard."

However, even *Ultrasaurus* may not have been the biggest sauropod dinosaur. Very recently,

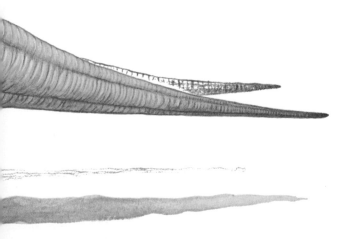

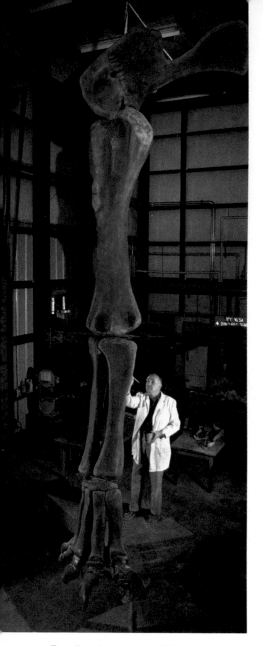

Dr. Jim Jensen of Brigham Young University in Provo, Utah, is shown standing next to the *Ultrasaurus* leg bones that he discovered in Colorado in 1979.

bones were found of a sauropod that has been named *Seismosaurus* (syz muh SAWR uhs), or "earth-shaker lizard." It may have been as much as 120 feet (37 m) long! And footprints of what seems to have been an even bigger sauropod dinosaur have been found in Morocco, in North Africa. It may have been 160 feet (49 m) in length!

Brachiosaurus fossils have been found in Colorado, in the United States, and in Algeria and Tanzania, in Africa. Other kinds of brachiosaurids have been found in Colorado, Texas, and Maryland, in the United States, as well as in England, western Europe, Australia, China, and several parts of Africa. These gigantic dinosaurs were apparently quite common throughout the world for millions of years.

Mamenchisaurus

(mah mehn chee SAWR uhs)

Mamenchisaurus was a sauropod dinosaur that lived in what is now China. Its name means "Mamenchi lizard," after the place in China—Mamenchi—where the fossil skeleton was discovered.

A *Mamenchisaurus* was as much as 72 feet (22 meters) long. But almost half of that length was made up of an enormous neck. The neck alone was about 33 feet (10 m) long—longer than the body of most dinosaurs! Memenchisauruses had the longest neck of any known creature that has ever lived.

The bones in a *Mamenchisaurus*'s neck fitted together in a way that must have kept the neck very stiff. Some scientists think this means that a *Mamenchisaurus* couldn't have lifted its neck. They think these dinosaurs must have stayed in water most of the time, with their necks floating on the surface. By simply swinging its head from side to side, a *Mamenchisaurus* could have fed easily on the tops of plants growing in the water.

Other scientists think that *Mamenchisaurus*'s
stiff neck shows that it was a land animal. If a
Mamenchisaurus could have stood up on its back
legs, its stiff neck would have swung straight up,
lifting its head a good 50 feet (15 m) into the air.
This would have enabled a *Mamenchisaurus* to

feed off the leaves at the very tops of trees, which most other dinosaurs couldn't have reached.

There are reasons, then, for thinking *Mamenchisaurus* was a water-dwelling animal, as well as reasons for thinking it was a land-dwelling one. At the moment, no one knows which it was.

Compsognathus
(kahmp suh NAY thuhs)

About 150 million years ago, a very small dinosaur prowled through a forest that grew along the shore of a sea covering part of what is now Germany. It was no bigger than a chicken. But to smaller animals, it must have seemed as ferocious as a big *Ceratosaurus* would have seemed to a *Camptosaurus*. This sharp-toothed, fast-moving meat-eater was built like a giant carnosaur!

This dinosaur has been named *Compsognathus*, which means something like "pretty jaw." It is one of the smallest dinosaurs we know of, only 2 feet (60 centimeters) long. It was slimly built, and

weighed only about 6½ pounds (3 kilograms).

Compsognathus's sharp little teeth show that it was a meat-eater. And we actually know the kinds of animals it ate. A fossil Compsognathus skeleton found in Germany contained a number of tiny bones where the Compsognathus's stomach would have been. A scientist found that these were the bones of a small, long-tailed lizard that the Compsognathus had swallowed whole.

This also tells us that a Compsognathus was a fast, skillful hunter. Lizards can often move very quickly, so a Compsognathus must have been quite fast-running and quick-moving to be able to catch these creatures. Compsognathus fossils have been found in both Germany and France.

Other animals of the Jurassic Period

During the Jurassic Period, two of the "new" kinds of animals that first appeared during the Triassic Period increased and multiplied. One kind was the furry mammal. Some mammals were now cat-sized animals that probably scurried through the underbrush, keeping out of the dinosaurs' way. By the end of the Jurassic Period there were tree-dwelling mammals that looked very much like the squirrels of today.

The other kind of animal was the pterosaur, or flying reptile. *Dimorphodon* (dy MAWR fuh dahn), meaning "two shapes of teeth," was a pterosaur that lived in the early Jurassic. It was about 3 feet (1 meter) long, with a big head and long, snaky tail. *Rhamphorhynchus* (ram fuh RIHNG kuhs), meaning "prow beak," which lived somewhat later, was smaller and slimmer. It, too, had a long tail, with a leaf-shaped flap of skin at the end. This may have served as a rudder to help *Rhamphorhynchus* steer itself as it flew.

Pterodactylus (tehr uh DAK tuh luhs), or "winged finger," lived at about the same time as *Rhamphorhynchus*. It was about the size of a sparrow, and had no tail. The wings of all these creatures were long, pointed flaps of skin. The skin

Dimorphodon

Pterodactylus

Rhamphorhynchus

was attached to the arms and the fourth fingers of their hands, and to the body back to the hips. Pterosaurs flew by flapping their wings, as birds do.

The reptiles of today are cold-blooded and scaly. Even though the pterosaurs were reptiles, they may have been warm-blooded, as are mammals. The larger pterosaurs, such as *Dimorphodon*, probably ate fish. They could catch their prey by skimming over the water of lakes or streams and snatching up a fish in their jaws. Smaller pterosaurs, such as *Pterodactylus*, probably ate insects that they caught as they flew.

In the seas, the ichthyosaurs, or "fish-lizards," continued to flourish throughout the Jurassic Period. They were joined by new creatures known as plesiosaurs (PLEE see uh sawrz) or "near lizards." These animals may have been descendants of the Triassic nothosaurs.

There were two kinds of plesiosaurs. One kind had a big, bulky body, a short tail, four flippers, and a long neck with a small head. The other kind had a short neck and large, long head. The long-necked plesiosaurs probably swam near the surface of the water and preyed on fish. Short-necked plesiosaurs probably dived down to the sea bottom to prey on large octopuslike creatures. Both kinds of plesiosaurs were about 10

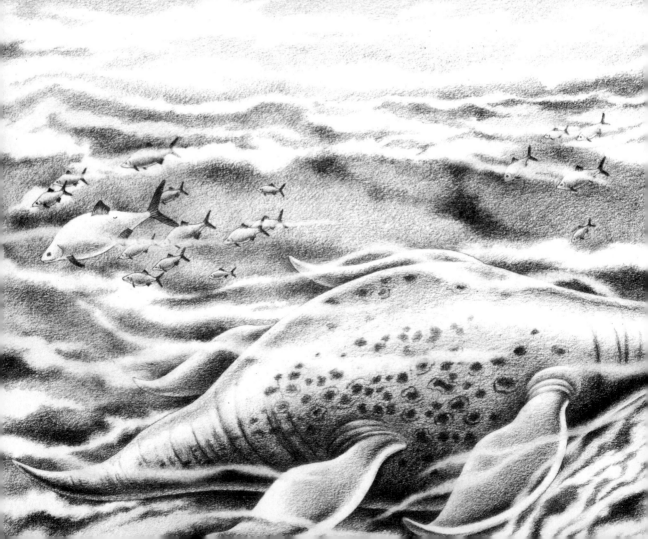

feet (3 m) long. By now, there were also several kinds of crocodilians (krahk uh DIHL ee uhnz), or creatures like crocodiles, living both on land and in the sea. One kind of sea-going crocodilian had four flippers and a fin on its tail. Some of the land crocodilians that often went into water to get food had pointed tails, long slim jaws, and webbed feet. They were as much as 20 feet (6 m) long.

The only Jurassic bird that is well known lived toward the end of the period. It was actually very much like the little two-legged dinosaur

long-necked plesiosaur

short-necked plesiosaur

Archaeopteryx

Compsognathus. It had a long snaky tail, arms with clawed hands, and sharp little teeth in its long, lizardlike jaws. However, feathers covered its body, it had big feathers on each side of its tail, and it had several layers of feathers on its arms, forming wings. The way the feathers were formed shows that this animal could fly. It was definitely a bird.

This creature has been named *Archaeopteryx* (ahr kee AHP tuhr ihks), meaning "ancient wing." Because *Archaeopteryx* and other ancient birds were so much like little dinosaurs, most scientists believe that birds are probably descended from dinosaurs.

An *Archaeopteryx* probably couldn't fly very

well. Many scientists think these birds may have climbed trees and then leaped into the air, snapping at flying insects as they flapped and fluttered to the ground. Others think that *Archaeopteryx* may have been a much better flier than that.

Archaeopteryx was probably not an ancestor of any bird of today. Archaeopteryxes probably died out without leaving any descendants. However, there must have been many other kinds of birds during the Jurassic Period. And, along with mammals, crocodilians, ichthyosaurs, and plesiosaurs, they continued to increase and multiply as the Jurassic Period came to an end.

Dinosaurs of the Cretaceous Period

Opossums first appeared during the heyday of the dinosaurs.

The Heyday of the Dinosaurs

By the end of the period during which the Jura rocks formed, many shallow seas had spread over parts of the land. In these seas lived trillions of tiny shelled animals.

For millions of years, trillions upon trillions of these animals died and sank to the sea bottom. Their shells, piled up by the hundreds of tons, were squeezed together and formed layers of chalk. So, scientists have named this period during which the chalk formed the Cretaceous (krih TAY shuhs) Period. The name means "chalk containing."

During the Cretaceous Period, which lasted from 144 million to 65 million years ago, tremendous changes of all kinds took place. Huge areas of land which had been joined together slowly moved apart and began to form the continents of today. New seas flowed into places where dinosaurs had once roamed.

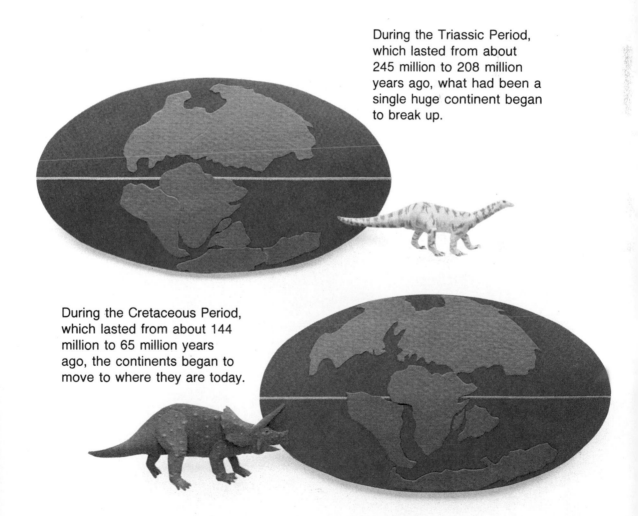

During the Triassic Period, which lasted from about 245 million to 208 million years ago, what had been a single huge continent began to break up.

During the Cretaceous Period, which lasted from about 144 million to 65 million years ago, the continents began to move to where they are today.

There was an enormous change in plant life. The tropical forests of ferns and palmlike trees slowly became smaller. Forests of trees that are common in the world today—oaks, poplars, willows, magnolias, and others—took over. Grapevines and other flowering plants that bore fruit also appeared.

With flowers spreading over the earth, many kinds of insects began to use them for food, and slowly changed as a result. Bees and butterflies appeared in the world and quickly increased.

Other kinds of creatures increased and did well,

too. Pterosaurs, the flying reptiles, grew in size until some of them had a wingspread of 40 feet (12 meters). Birds multiplied until, by the end of the period, there were many different kinds, large and small. Mammals also increased. Although they stayed small, many new kinds appeared. One was an animal much like the opossum of today.

But the Cretaceous Period was, most

of all, the heyday, or best time, for the dinosaurs.
A great many new kinds of dinosaurs appeared
and became numerous during the period. The main
reason for this was that the new plants provided
an enormous food supply for certain kinds of
dinosaurs. These kinds were able to increase
tremendously, while some other kinds of dinosaurs
that had depended on the older plants slowly died
off.

Many kinds of duckbilled dinosaurs, horned
dinosaurs, armored dinosaurs, and others appeared.
All of these dinosaurs multiplied and spread
throughout the world. And the great number of
plant-eaters provided a big food supply for the
many new kinds of meat-eaters that appeared.

So the dinosaurs did very well throughout the
Cretaceous Period. It was truly their heyday. But
it was also their finish. For, with the end of the
period, all the many different kinds of dinosaurs,
as well as a number of other kinds of creatures,
became extinct. What caused this to happen is one
of the greatest scientific mysteries.

Hypsilophodon
(hihp suh LAHF uh dahn)

Hypsilophodons were small ornithopod, or "bird-footed," plant-eaters. They were from 4½ to 7½ feet (1.4–2.3 meters) long. But half of a *Hypsilophodon*'s length was made up of its long stiff tail. These animals were very fast runners—perhaps the fastest of all dinosaurs. They ran on their toes, with their tails stretched straight out for balance. Running away was their only defense against meat-eaters.

Hypsilophodon means "high-ridged tooth." These animals were given this name because their teeth were shaped like triangles with a high point, or ridge, and bumpy edges. A *Hypsilophodon* had a row of teeth along each side of its jaws and a few teeth in the front of its jaws in a hard beak, like the beak of a bird. It snipped off plant stems and leaves with its beak and chewed them up with

its side teeth. As a *Hypsilophodon*'s teeth wore out, new ones grew in to replace them.

Unlike reptiles of today, hypsilophodons had cheeks. Thus a *Hypsilophodon* could hold a lot of food in its mouth while slowly chewing it. This was very useful in case a *Hypsilophodon* had to suddenly run away from a good feeding place because a hungry meat-eater appeared. The *Hypsilophodon* could carry off a lot of food in its cheeks.

All these things—good teeth, cheeks, and the

ability to run very fast—helped *Hypsilophodon*
and its relatives, which are known as
hypsilophodontids (hihp suh lahf uh DAHN tihds), to
survive. These little dinosaurs lived on for about
100 million years, while many other kinds of
dinosaurs died out and new kinds appeared.

Hypsilophodon fossils have been found in
southern England and Portugal. Other
hypsilophodontids lived in what are now Australia,
Canada, eastern England, and Romania, as well as
in parts of Africa and the western United States.

Deinonychus
(dy noh NIHK uhs)

A plant-eating dinosaur some 20 feet (6 meters) long plodded through deep underbrush, making its way to a distant lake. It walked on all fours, but at times it stopped and stood up on its back legs to peer around in search of possible danger. When it was sure that it was safe, it dropped back onto all fours again and continued on its way.

But, one of the times when the animal stood up, it saw that it was no longer safe. A group of five other dinosaurs was coming toward it. And they were coming very fast!

The plant-eater broke into a run. If it could reach the lake it might be able to swim to safety. Although it moved surprisingly fast, it could not outrun the speedy beasts that were chasing it.

Long before it could reach the edge of the lake they had caught up to it.

The attackers ran on two legs, with their tails stretched straight out behind them. They were slim creatures, much smaller than the plant-eater. Their jaws were filled with rows of sharp teeth and they had sharp claws on their "hands" and feet. The first toe on each foot had a big, curved, razor-sharp claw that stuck straight up.

These little dinosaurs were meat-eaters, and now they attacked!

The plant-eater turned its body sideways and lashed its tail like a whip. A blow from that tail could have broken some of the small reptiles' bones, but they dodged aside. One of them sprang in close to the plant-eater and gave a savage kick with one of its feet. The sharp claw on its toe slashed into the plant-eater's side, making a long, deep, bloody wound.

The plant-eater whirled around and swung its tail again, but the little flesh-eater leaped out of reach. At the same instant, another of the small reptiles delivered another kick into the plant-eater's belly, tearing it open.

The plant-eater's legs gave way and it collapsed in a pool of blood. Instantly, the five small dinosaurs swarmed over it, giving it more vicious kicks. Each kick opened another terrible wound in the plant-eater's body. In a few minutes, it was dead.

A fight such as this may have taken place often in the western part of North America early in the Cretaceous Period. For that was where and when the small meat-eating dinosaurs that we call *Deinonychus*, or "terrible claw," lived. These creatures were probably the most fierce and deadly hunters of their time. There is some evidence that

they hunted in packs, much as wolves do today. They were probably very fast runners.

A *Deinonychus* was from 8 to 13 feet (2.4–4 m) long and about 5 feet (1.5 m) high. That's not very big. But the large, curved claw on each foot was a dreadful weapon that made these little dinosaurs very dangerous. A *Deinonychus* could seize its prey with its clawed hands and rip open the animal's body with a single kick!

Most reptiles of today have snaky, twisty tails, but a *Deinonychus*'s tail was always straight and stiff. The bones of the tail were locked together so that the tail could not curl. The straight, stiff tail helped a *Deinonychus* keep its balance as it raced after its prey, changing direction in an instant and leaping to make one of its deadly kicks.

A *Deinonychus* was a quick-moving, dangerous animal. We think of dinosaurs such as *Allosaurus* and *Tyrannosaurus* as fierce and terrible hunters, but the little *Deinonychus* may have been far more fierce and terrible!

Tenontosaurus

(tehn ahn tuh SAWR uhs)

Tenontosaurus was a middle-sized plant-eater that lived in western North America at the same time as *Deinonychus*. It was about 20 feet (6 meters) long, with a very long tail. It probably walked on all four feet most of the time.

There is some evidence that tenontosauruses

were hunted by packs of deinonychuses. The skeletons of a *Tenontosaurus* and five deinonychuses were found together. The *Tenontosaurus* might have killed the five little meat-eaters, but was then killed by other members of the hunting pack.

    Tenontosaurus means "tendon lizard." A tendon is a tough cord that connects a muscle to a bone in an animal's body.

Hylaeosaurus

(hy lee uh SAWR uhs)

The Isle of Wight is a small island that lies off the southern coast of England. At the beginning of the Cretaceous Period it was part of a mainland, and was the home of a four-legged, plant-eating dinosaur that has been named *Hylaeosaurus*, meaning "forest lizard."

Hylaeosaurus was one of the first kinds of nodosaurs (NOHD uh sawrs), or "knobby lizards." These dinosaurs had bumpy, bony armor covering parts of their bodies. *Hylaeosaurus* had bony, oval knobs embedded in the skin on its sides and back. A double row of bony spikes, like big horns, ran down its back, from neck to hips. Another double row of spikes ran down its tail.

It's easy to see that a *Hylaeosaurus* was well protected against attacks by carnosaurs. Even a big-toothed *Allosaurus* surely wouldn't have been able to bite through the bony knobs on a *Hylaeosaurus*'s body. And if a *Hylaeosaurus* simply pushed itself hard against a carnosaur's

body, the spikes on the back of the *Hylaeosaurus* could have made deep wounds. It might also have been able to badly hurt a carnosaur by swinging its spiky tail hard against the carnosaur's legs or body.

A *Hylaeosaurus* was about 13 feet (4 meters) long and weighed between 1 and 2 tons (0.9–1.8 metric tons). These animals had rather small, weak teeth. They probably lived in forests growing around swamps or lakes. In such places there would be plenty of soft plants they could easily bite through.

Iguanodon
(ih GWAHN uh dahn)

Iguanodons were plant-eating ornithopod
dinosaurs. They were descended from the
camptosaurs, which lived millions of years earlier
during the Jurassic Period. An *Iguanodon* was
much like a *Camptosaurus*, only bigger—as much
as 29 feet (8.8 meters) long and 16 feet (4.9 m)
high. The males were larger than the females.

Scientists have been able to find out quite a bit
about how these animals lived. They probably
stayed mostly in low, swampy land where there
were vast fields of the plants called horsetails that
grow near water. Iguanodons probably fed mostly

on these plants, which are quite tough and scratchy. The teeth in most *Iguanodon* skulls that have been found were worn down, as if from chewing such tough plants. Iguanodons probably walked on all four feet most of the time, and only reared up on their hind legs to get at high-growing plants.

Iguanodon means "iguana tooth." These dinosaurs were given this name because their teeth are much like the teeth of the iguana lizard of today, but much bigger. An *Iguanodon* had teeth only in the sides of its jaws. As these teeth wore out, new ones grew in to take their place. The front part of an *Iguanodon*'s mouth was a toothless beak, like a bird's beak, for snipping off plant stems.

More than a hundred years ago, some Belgian coal miners found that the rock they were digging in was full of huge bones. The bones turned out to be the skeletons of more than thirty iguanodons. Because so many skeletons were found together, some scientists think this shows that iguanodons lived in large herds. Something must have happened that caught this herd by surprise— perhaps a sudden flash flood—and killed all the animals.

Iguanodons were probably too big and bulky to move very fast, so they couldn't run from meat-eaters. But they may have been able to defend themselves. The "thumb" on each of an *Iguanodon*'s hands was a long, pointed spike of bone. This could have been used as a weapon against meat-eaters. A hard jab of one of those spikes into a meat-eater's eye or soft underbelly would have caused a serious wound. A herd of iguanodons ganging up on a carnosaur that tried to attack them could probably have killed the meat-eater.

Fossil remains of iguanodons have been found in all parts of the world. They were one of the most common kind of dinosaurs.

Ouranosaurus
(ur an uh SAWR uhs)

The Sahara is an enormous, sandy desert in North Africa, where the weather now is always hot and dry. But in the early part of the Cretaceous Period, about 120 million years ago, it was a great plain, crossed by rivers and covered with green plants. There was plenty of food there for plant-eating dinosaurs.

On one part of this plain, near a river, roamed herds of plant-eaters that have been named *Ouranosaurus*, meaning "brave lizard." They were ornithopod dinosaurs, very much like iguanodons—except for two things. For one thing, they had flat jaws like the bill of a duck or goose. For another, they had a kind of large, long fin running down the back and tail.

Scientists think this fin probably let a *Ouranosaurus* either warm up or cool off, whichever was needed. After a long, cool night, when a cold-blooded reptile's body is stiff and slow, a

Ouranosaurus might have turned sideways toward the sun.

This would have caused the fin to quickly soak up heat, warming the animal so that it could move more quickly and easily.

Then, during the hot part of the day, the *Ouranosaurus* might face the sun, so that no sunlight shone directly on the side of its fin. The fin could then radiate, or give off, stored-up heat from the *Ouranosaurus*'s body, cooling it off. Of course, a *Ouranosaurus* would do these things naturally, without understanding why it did them.

A *Ouranosaurus* was 23 feet (7 meters) long. These dinosaurs probably walked and ran on two legs. But to feed on the low-growing plants that covered the plain, they probably stood on all four legs.

Psittacosaurus

(siht uh kuh SAWR uhs)

One hundred ten million years ago, a little group of two-legged dinosaurs moved slowly through a forest in what is now eastern China. They had long arms and four-fingered hands tipped with stubby claws. Their heads looked much like the head of a parrot, for the jaws formed a beak such as parrots have. A short, bony frill stuck out from the back of the head.

The largest of these dinosaurs was about 5 feet (1.5 meters) long and 2½ feet (0.75 m) high. The others were no more than 10 inches (25 centimeters) long. The large one was a mother and the small ones were her young. They kept close beside her, watching carefully as she dropped to all fours to feed off a leafy, low-growing plant. Her sharp beak sliced through the tough leaves like a

scissors. The little ones imitated her, biting off tiny bits of leaf with their small beaks.

This kind of dinosaur has been named *Psittacosaurus*, which means "parrot lizard." It was given this name because its beak looks like a parrot's beak. It was a new kind of dinosaur. Its ancestors were probably ornithopods such as *Hypsilophodon*, but it was one of the first kind of dinosaurs we call ceratopsians, or horned dinosaurs. While *Psittacosaurus* itself did not have a horn, most of its relatives that lived many millions of years later were horned.

Psittacosauruses were heavily built and were probably rather slow-moving. They don't seem to have had any kind of defense, so they may have stayed inside thick forests where they would be safe from big carnosaurs that roamed the open country.

A number of fossil skeletons of young psittacosauruses have been found. All had slightly worn teeth, probably from chewing the same kinds of tough plants that a grown-up *Psittacosaurus* ate. We don't know for sure if young psittacosauruses really stayed with their mothers, but they probably did.

Psittacosaurus fossils have also been found in Mongolia and in southern Siberia, in the Soviet Union.

Protoceratops
(proh toh SEHR uh tahps)

A small herd of dinosaurs was feeding on clumps of plants that dotted a broad sandy plain. They were squat, bulky reptiles, no more than 6 feet (1.8 meters) long, with a thick tail and stout legs. The mouth formed a pointed, sharp-edged beak that easily snipped through tough plant stems. The back of the skull flared out into a broad shield of bone that protected the back and shoulders.

One of these dinosaurs, a female, began to nose about in the sandy soil. When she found a spot that suited her, she began to dig. Using the stubby claws on her five-toed front legs, she soon scooped out a broad, round, shallow pit.

Then, moving around so as to place herself over the pit, she began to lay eggs. As each egg dropped into the pit, she shuffled a step or two sideways so that the next egg fell beside the one before it. After a time, more than a dozen long eggs with wrinkly shells lay in a winding circle in the pit.

With her back legs the female kicked sand over the eggs until they were lightly covered. The heat of the sun baking down on the sand would hatch

the eggs. Meanwhile, the herd of plant-eaters would browse nearby, guarding the eggs and the young that finally hatched. While these small dinosaurs had neither sharp teeth nor sharp claws, their beaks were good weapons.

These small plant-eaters lived from 80 million to 100 million years ago in what is now the Gobi, a desert in Mongolia. Although they did not have horns, they were among the ancestors of a large family of dinosaurs that were horned—the ceratopsids, or "horned faces"—that lived millions

of years later. And so, scientists named these dinosaurs *Protoceratops,* or "first horned face."

We know exactly how a *Protoceratops* laid its eggs and what the eggs were like because a fossilized nest of *Protoceratops* eggs was found in 1924. These were the first dinosaur eggs ever found, and they proved that dinosaurs, like reptiles of today, hatched from eggs. The eggs were about the size and shape of a large baked potato. The shells were hard, like the shell of a chicken egg, but very wrinkly instead of smooth.

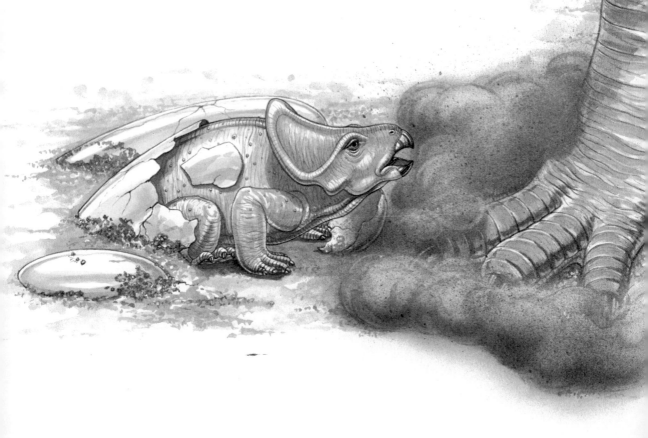

Spinosaurus
(spy noh SAWR uhs)

About 80 million years ago, the land that is now the country of Egypt was the home of some rather unusual carnosaurs. These were large animals, 40 feet (12 meters) long, with a big head and a mouth full of sharp teeth. They looked much like an *Allosaurus* or *Tyrannosaurus*. But they were quite different from those carnosaurs, and others, in two ways. For one thing, their teeth were straight, instead of curved like the teeth of all other carnosaurs. For another thing, they had a kind of big fin, more than 6 feet (1.8 m) high, on the back.

This fin was formed by long, slim bones on the animal's spine. Thin skin, filled with blood vessels, stretched over the bones. This dinosaur has been named *Spinosaurus,* or "spine lizard."

Spinosaurus lived in very open country where it was probably exposed to bright, hot sunshine much of the time. Because of this, scientists think that *Spinosaurus*'s fin was probably a device for helping it warm up or cool off, as needed. In the morning, after a cool night had drained much of the warmth out of its body, a *Spinosaurus* could have warmed up quickly just by lying with one side of its fin facing the sun so as to soak up heat. Later in the day, when the animal might have begun to get too hot, it could have cooled off by lying down facing away from the sun so that no light shone directly on either side of its fin. The fin would have soon begun giving off heat and the *Spinosaurus*'s body would have gradually cooled.

However, having that large, stiff, probably rather brittle fin on its back would have made it rather difficult for a *Spinosaurus* to fight. So it probably wasn't a hunter that got its prey by leaping on it and clawing and biting it to death. More than likely, a *Spinosaurus* seldom if ever killed anything itself. It probably stalked about looking for dead animals on which to feed.

Spinosaurus was actually the last and biggest of a whole group of carnosaurs with fins. A smaller finned carnosaur, called *Altispinax* (al tih SPYN aks), meaning "high spine," lived in northwest Europe in the early part of the Cretaceous Period. And an even smaller one was called *Metriacanthosaurus* (meht ruh uh kan thuh SAWR uhs), or "somewhat high-spined lizard." It lived during the Jurassic Period in what is now England. This small, finned carnosaur was probably the ancestor of *Spinosaurus* and all the others.

Hypselosaurus
(hihp sehl uh SAWR uhs)

The long-necked, long-tailed sauropod dinosaurs were, of course, the biggest kind of dinosaur. They were sometimes more than 100 feet (30 meters) long, and often weighed more than several elephants. However, a good many kinds of sauropod dinosaurs were much smaller. One of the smaller kind was *Hypselosaurus.*

The name *Hypselosaurus* means "high lizard." But these dinosaurs weren't really very high, and were only about 40 feet (12 m) long. There wasn't anything very special about them, but they are of importance to people interested in dinosaurs. This is because they are the only one of the sauropod dinosaurs we know of whose eggs have been found.

A *Hypselosaurus* egg was about 10 or 12 inches (25–30 centimeters) long. This is probably about as big as any dinosaur egg could be. The baby that hatched out of such an egg weighed only about 2 pounds (1 kilogram), or much less than a newborn human baby. However, a full-grown

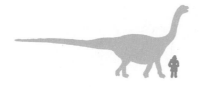

Hypselosaurus weighed around 20,000 pounds (9,000 kg). So, when a *Hypselosaurus* was fully grown, it had increased in size about ten thousand times. Sauropods of the bigger kind must have increased even more! (A human increases only about 20 to 25 times.)

Unlike most bird eggs of today, which are smooth, *Hypselosaurus* eggs were covered with small bumps. The eggs were probably white or cream-colored. Some *Hypselosaurus* eggs have been found in groups of five, so perhaps that's how many eggs a mother *Hypselosaurus* laid at one time.

Hypselosauruses lived in what is now France and Spain.

Velociraptor
(vuh lahs uh RAP tawr)

On two long, slim legs, a small, meat-eating dinosaur trotted over a flat, sandy plain. From nose to tail, it was about 6 feet (1.8 meters) long. Its slender tail stuck straight out behind it, and its long, narrow head turned this way and that as it peered about. On each of its feet, one large, sharp, curved claw stuck straight up.

Suddenly, the meat-eater broke into a run. It had caught sight of another creature in the distance. It raced across the plain at tremendous speed.

The other creature was a four-footed dinosaur. It, too, was no more than 6 feet (1.8 m) long, but it had thick legs, a bulky body and stout tail. It was a plant-eater, with no claws or sharp teeth.

But it did have a sharp, pointed beak. And a broad shield of bone grew out of the back of its skull and spread over its shoulders and back.

Looking up, the plant-eater saw the meat-eater racing toward it. Too slow to run away, the plant-eater made ready to fight. It stood with its legs spread and its beak open in defiance.

The meat-eater sped straight at its prey, but at the last moment swerved slightly to one side. With the swiftness of an eye-blink, it gave a hard kick with one of its feet. The sharp, curved claw on its foot ripped into the plant-eater's back and tore a long, deep gash across its shoulder and neck.

This was how the meat-eater usually killed its prey—with slashing kicks that crippled and weakened. But now, something went wrong. The big claw on the meat-eater's foot got stuck under the plant-eater's bony shield. The meat-eater was unable to pull its leg free!

The plant-eater turned its head and found that its enemy was within reach. The plant-eater's powerful jaws and sharp beak could slice through the toughest plants. Now it used jaws and beak to savagely bite into the meat-eater's body. The meat-eater struggled, slashing with the claw on its free leg. But the plant-eater held on, biting deep into its enemy's chest.

Then, as the animals thrashed about on the

ground, they suddenly rolled into a patch of quicksand. In moments they were buried under the sand and died, still locked together. Buried beneath the sand for millions of years, their bones became fossils. Scientists discovered the two skeletons in 1971.

We don't really know if a fight actually took place between the two animals. But from the way the skeletons lay, it certainly looks as if the meat-eater's claw had been caught under the plant-eater's shield. And the plant-eater's beak did seem to be biting into the meat-eater's chest.

We don't know what the two might have been fighting about, either. Perhaps the meat-eater did want to make a meal of the plant-eater. Or, perhaps the meat-eater had tried to steal the eggs in the plant-eater's nest and the plant-eater had attacked the meat-eater to protect the eggs.

The plant-eater was a *Protoceratops*. The meat-eater has been named *Velociraptor*, meaning "swift thief." Velociraptors lived about 80 million years ago, in what is now Mongolia, China, and part of southern Russia.

Ankylosaurus

(an KY luh sawr uhs)

Some of the most common dinosaurs that lived near the end of the Cretaceous Period were bulky, heavy, four-footed plant-eaters that were built like a battle tank! The head, back, and tail of these animals were covered with a flexible armor of bone slabs and knobs beneath tough, thick skin. They are known as ankylosaurids (an KY luh sawr ihds), meaning "fused lizards." This is because the bony pieces forming their armor were fused, or grown together.

The ankylosaurid that the whole family was named after was *Ankylosaurus.* It was about 33 feet (10 meters) long. It probably didn't fear even a *Tyrannosaurus.* If attacked, it had only to crouch down, pressing itself against the ground. There would have been nothing for the attacker to bite or claw at but thick, hard armor. The attacker might try to turn the *Ankylosaurus* over on its back, to get at its soft underside, but

Ankylosaurus and most other ankylosaurids were much too heavy for even a big *Tyrannosaurus* to move. In time, the attacker would probably just go away.

However, an ankylosaurid didn't have to wait for attackers to leave—it could drive them off. An ankylosaurid's tail was tipped with a big, heavy ball of bone that turned the tail into a war club! A vicious swing of such a tail could knock even a big carnosaur off its feet, and perhaps break some of its bones. So, altogether, ankylosaurids were probably well able to defend themselves, which may be why they were so common.

An ankylosaurid's mouth was like a hard beak, and farther back in its jaws were tiny, weak teeth. These animals must have fed on very soft low-growing plants. They probably lived on plains, where the ground was covered with plants and was hard enough to support their heavy weight.

Ankylosaurus lived in what is now Alberta, Canada, and Montana. A smaller ankylosaurid called *Euoplocephalus* (yoo uh pluh SEHF uh luhs), meaning "well-armored head," lived in Alberta, Canada, and northwest China. A good many other ankylosaurids have also been found in North America, China, and Mongolia.

Struthiomimus

(stroo thee oh MY muhs)

About a hundred years ago, when scientists began to study the bones of a newly discovered dinosaur, they quickly realized that it must have looked a lot like a creature that lives today—the ostrich. It was almost exactly the same size as an ostrich, and had a long neck and small head with a toothless beak, just as an ostrich does. It had long, slim legs, much like those of an ostrich. Of course, instead of wings it had long, slender arms and hands, and instead of tail feathers it had a long, snaky tail.

In time, fossils of several different kinds of these dinosaurs were discovered. The creatures were given names such as *Struthiomimus*, or "ostrich imitator"; *Ornithomimus* (awr nuh thuh MY muhs), or "bird imitator"; and *Gallimimus* (gal uh MY muhs), or "fowl imitator." This group of dinosaurs became known as "ostrich dinosaurs."

The ostrich dinosaur called *Struthiomimus* lived in what is now western Canada, in open country along rivers and streams. It was about 11 feet (3.4

Struthiomimus

meters) long and stood about 8 feet (2.4 m) high. It had strong arms and hands with sharp, curved claws. Perhaps it used its hands to snatch up lizards and other small creatures, and to hold dinosaur eggs while it sucked their contents after breaking the shells with a sharp blow of its hard beak. It probably also ate insects, fruit, and some plants.

Ornithomimus apparently lived a little later than *Struthiomimus*, and seems to have had a different way of life. It lived in thick, gloomy cypress swamp forests in what is now Colorado and Montana. Its arms were thinner and its hands weaker than those of *Struthiomimus*. It probably fed on insects, small animals, fruits, and plants of

the forest floor. It was about the same size as *Struthiomimus*.

Gallimimus was the biggest of the ostrich dinosaurs, about 13 feet (4 m) long. Its hands were clumsier than those of *Struthiomimus* and *Ornithomimus*, and probably couldn't have held things as well. However, its hands might have made good shovels for scraping sand or earth, so perhaps it fed mostly on dinosaur eggs that it dug up. *Gallimimus* lived in what is now Mongolia.

All these ostrich dinosaurs were very fast. They could probably run faster than a galloping horse! This was their only defense against huge carnosaurs such as *Tyrannosaurus*, which lived at the same time.

Ornithomimus

Deinocheirus
(dy nuh KY ruhs)

In 1965, an expedition of fossil hunters went to the Gobi, a desert in Mongolia, in search of dinosaur fossils. They found something that was new, astounding, and a complete mystery!

What they found were the arm bones of an unknown kind of dinosaur that had lived in Mongolia 70 or 80 million years ago. The bones are astounding because they are enormous. Each arm is larger than a tall person. The huge clawed hands on the arms could have picked up a person the way a person picks up a kitten!

The dinosaur with these great arms and big hands has been named *Deinocheirus*, which means "terrible hand." The mystery is, what kind of dinosaur was *Deinocheirus*, and just how big was it?

From the look of its clawed hands, *Deinocheirus* was a meat-eater. The big meat-eating carnosaurs, such as *Tyrannosaurus*, had tiny arms for their size. If *Deinocheirus* was a carnosaur, and its arms were small for its size, it must have been an enormous creature—one of the biggest of all two-legged dinosaurs.

But many scientists think *Deinocheirus* was probably an ostrich dinosaur, like *Struthiomimus*. Most ostrich dinosaurs weren't very big—only

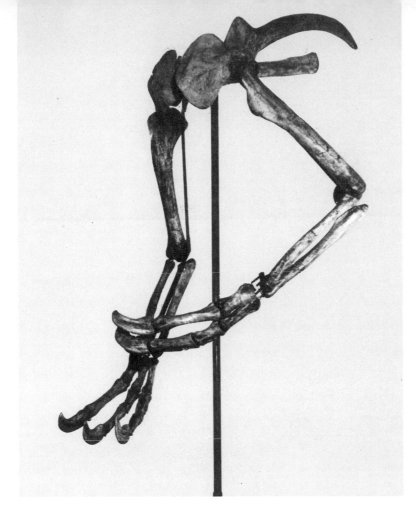

The girl *(right)* is shown in proper size to the
arms of the dinosaur named "terrible hand."

about 14 feet (4.3 meters) long—and had rather
long arms in proportion to their bodies. So, if
Deinocheirus was an ostrich dinosaur, it was
probably about 40 feet (12.2 m) long. That's
certainly big, but not as big as many other
dinosaurs.

Was *Deinocheirus* a gigantic "super" dinosaur,
or just a very big ostrich dinosaur? We won't know
for sure until more "terrible hand" bones are
found.

Dromiceiomimus
(droh mih see oh MY muhs)

As the red evening sun went down, twilight began
to close over the woods. Black shadows thickened
among the trees, and the forest floor darkened.
Now the many little creatures that had stayed
hidden during the day came out to seek food. One
of them—a small, furry, mouselike mammal—
emerged from its hiding place among some bushes.
Nose twitching, it crept out onto the forest floor,
ready to dart for cover if anything stirred.

Back among the shadows a much larger creature stood patiently, not moving a muscle. Its large, glittering eyes watched for a sign of movement on the forest floor. Then it caught sight of the creeping mammal. In an instant, it shot out of hiding. The mammal had time for only a single squeak of fright before a birdlike head pecked down and gulped it up!

The creature that had caught the mammal was a rather small, slim dinosaur that has been given the name *Dromiceiomimus*, meaning "emu imitator." (An emu is an ostrichlike Australian bird.) *Dromiceiomimus* was one of the "ostrich dinosaurs," but seems to have had a different way

of life from the others. It lived in woodlands in what is now part of Canada. Because it had the largest eyes of any land-dwelling animal, scientists think it could probably see very well in dim twilight or moonlight. Thus, it probably did all its hunting around sunset, when the little animals that stayed hidden all day came out.

Fossils of both adult and young dromiceiomimuses have been found together. This seems to show that these dinosaurs may have looked after their young ones in much the same way that ostriches and emus do today. Perhaps the young dromiceiomimuses stayed with their parents, learning how to hunt and care for themselves, until they were big enough to go off on their own.

A full-grown *Dromiceiomimus* was only about 11½ feet (3.3 meters) long, and had no teeth or large claws. So, like the other ostrich dinosaurs, its only defense was to run away. But it probably did that very well. From the way its body was formed, scientists think *Dromiceiomimus* was probably the fastest of all dinosaurs. It was probably also one of the smartest, for it had a good-sized brain for the size of its head.

Oviraptor

(oh vuh RAP tawr)

Oviraptors were small dinosaurs with short heads. Their jaws formed a short, curved beak with a small, stubby horn at the end. They had no teeth. They ran about on two legs and had three-fingered hands that could pick up things and hold them. Oviraptors may have had feathers on parts of their bodies, such as the back of the neck.

An *Oviraptor* skeleton was found beside a nest of *Protoceratops* eggs. Some scientists think this shows that these dinosaurs may have fed on dinosaur eggs that they dug up out of nests. This is why they were given their name, which means "egg thief."

Other scientists aren't so sure about this. The way an *Oviraptor*'s beak and jaws are formed shows that it had a powerful, crushing bite—far more powerful than would have been needed to crack an eggshell. So, some scientists think that oviraptors may have lived mainly on clams or other shellfish with hard shells that an *Oviraptor* could crack open with its beak.

From the front of its beak to the tip of its tail an *Oviraptor* was about 6 feet (1.8 meters) long. These dinosaurs lived in what is now southern Mongolia.

Monoclonius
(mahn uh KLOHN ee uhs)

Some 70 or 80 million years ago, large herds of four-legged, plant-eating dinosaurs roamed over what is now North America. They were bulky, heavy animals, about 18 feet (5.5 meters) long, with huge heads. Out of the back of the skull grew a broad shield of bone that spread back over the shoulders. Over the nostrils, they had a long, pointed horn.

These creatures were one of the big family of
ceratopsids (sehr uh TAHP sihds), or "horned
faces." Because of their single horn, scientists
named them *Monoclonius*, meaning "one-horned."

Monoclonius herds moved about on the plains
and in the woodlands at the edges of forests. The
animals cropped low-growing plants with their
beaklike mouth. It is doubtful that a carnosaur,

even a large *Tyrannosaurus*, would have dared to attack such a herd. Groups of monocloniuses probably would have charged at it and stabbed it to death with their horns!

During the last few million years of the Cretaceous Period, ceratopsids were very numerous. There were *Monoclonius* herds all the way from what is now Alberta, Canada, down to what is now Mexico. There were several different species, or kinds, of monocloniuses, just as there are now different species of bears, cats, and other creatures.

There were also herds of other kinds of ceratopsids, related to *Monoclonius* but somewhat different in appearance. One of these was *Centrosaurus* (sehn truh SAWR uhs), or "sharp-pointed lizard." Like *Monoclonius*, it had a nose horn, but the horn was bent forward. Some scientists think *Centrosaurus* was really just another kind of *Monoclonius*. It was about 20 feet (6 m) long.

Another relative was *Styracosaurus* (sty rak uh SAWR uhs), or "spiked lizard." It, too, had a long nose horn, and two small horns over its eyes. But it gets its name from the six long, sharp spikes sticking up out of its bony head shield. A *Styracosaurus* was about 18 feet (5.5 m) long.

A rather strange sort of ceratopsid was *Pachyrhinosaurus* (pak uh ry noh SAWR uhs), or

Centrosaurus

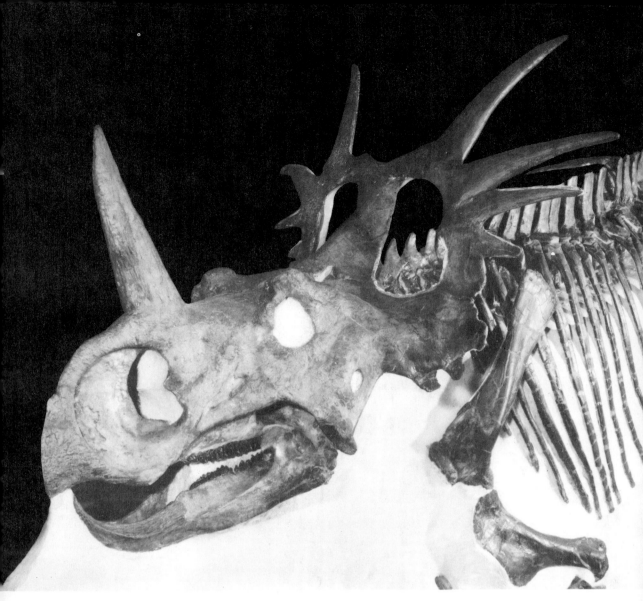

This *Styracosaurus* skeleton shows the six sharp spikes sticking up out of the head shield, and the long nose horn.

"thick-nosed lizard." While this horned dinosaur had stubby horns on its head shield, it had none on its nose or forehead. Instead, it had a thick, rough patch of bone on its forehead.

Scientists think male pachyrhinosauruses may have fought one another at mating time by butting their foreheads together, as goats do. The bony pads would have protected them from injury, but sooner or later one would have given up and the other would be the winner.

Pachyrhinosauruses had thick, bony patches instead of horns on their heads. They probably used these in fights with one another.

Triceratops
(try SEHR uh tahps)

One of the last and biggest of the ceratopsids is a rather famous dinosaur—*Triceratops,* or "three-horned face." A *Triceratops* had two long, curved, sharp horns projecting out above its eyes and a short, sharp horn on its nose. It was as much as 30 feet (9 meters) long and weighed as much as 6 tons (5.4 metric tons).

Triceratops is very well known. Many dinosaurs are known from only a few bones, but we have found hundreds of *Triceratops* skulls and bones. Scientists think these animals must have been very common during the last few million years of the Cretaceous Period. Enormous herds of them may have roamed over much of what is now the western part of North America.

The triceratopses in each herd may have been slightly different from those in every other herd. Scientists have found that there may have been as many as fifteen species, or kinds, of these dinosaurs. Each species was just a little different from the others. For example, one species was bigger than all others, while another was smaller. One species had straight horns instead of curved ones. One species had no nose horn.

One way scientists can tell that these were all truly triceratopses and not other kinds of

ceratopsids is by the frill, or bony shield, growing
out of the skull. All other ceratopsid dinosaurs had
large holes in their bony frills, but a *Triceratops*'s
frill was solid. Thus, any skull with a solid frill is a
Triceratops skull.

There doesn't seem much doubt that a
Triceratops used its frill as a shield. The frills of

some *Triceratops* skulls are marred by deep scars and scratches. However, these marks weren't made by the claws or teeth of carnosaurs, but by the horns of other triceratopses! These creatures must have fought each other often, jerking and twisting their heads to jab and push with their horns!

Perhaps only the males fought at mating time, as some male goats, deer, and other horned creatures do today. Such fights weren't to kill, but just to show which animal was strongest—and that was the one that won a mate. Some of these struggles must have been hard-fought, because the skull of one *Triceratops* that was found had a

This *Triceratops* skull is in the National Museum in Washington, D.C.

broken horn. It was probably broken against the shield of another *Triceratops*, in a fight.

Although we have found a good many more skulls and bones of *Triceratops* than of most other dinosaurs, there are still many things we don't know about these creatures. We don't know if they held their tails out straight or let them drag. We don't know if they had spread-out toes or if they had round, flat feet like an elephant. And while some scientists think a *Triceratops* was probably very slow-moving, others think it might have been able to gallop as fast as 30 miles (48 kilometers) per hour!

Torosaurus

(toh roh SAWR uhs)

Monoclonius, *Styracosaurus*, *Centrosaurus*, and *Triceratops* were all short-frilled ceratopsids. Their bony shields, or frills, reached back only to their shoulders. But there was also a large group of long-frilled ceratopsids. The bony shields of some of these horned dinosaurs reached halfway back to their hips!

Such huge pieces of bone would have been very heavy if they had been solid like the shield of a *Triceratops*. But, like the frills of most of the short-frilled ceratopsids, the frills of long-frilled ceratopsids had large holes in them to make them lighter. The animals' tough skin covered the holes.

Of course, a shield with holes in it certainly isn't as much protection as a solid shield. But scientists don't think long-frilled ceratopsids used their shields only for protection—they were probably also used to frighten an enemy. When a long-frilled ceratopsid lowered its head, its huge frill would have been lifted straight up. This would have made it seem as if the animal had suddenly become larger, which might have frightened an attacker away.

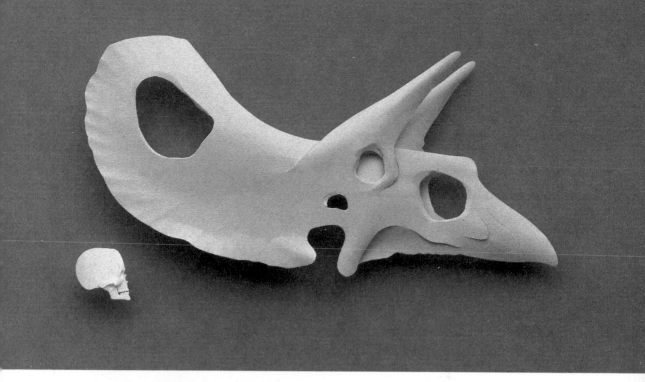

A human skull next to a *Torosaurus* skull shows what a gigantic head a *Torosaurus* had—the largest head of any animal that has ever lived on land.

To support such a big frill, a long-frilled ceratopsid had an enormous head. One of the biggest of them, *Torosaurus*, or "bull lizard," had the biggest head of any animal that has ever lived on land. From the tip of its beaked mouth to the end of its frill, a *Torosaurus* skull was as much as 8½ feet (2.6 meters) long.

Altogether, a *Torosaurus* was about 25 feet (7.6 m) long and weighed 8 to 9 tons (7.3–8.2 metric tons). It had two long horns above its eyes and a very short horn on its nose. *Torosaurus* fossils have been found in Alberta, Canada.

Pentaceratops (pehn tuh SEHR uh tahps), or "five-horned face," was another long-frilled

ceratopsid. Like *Torosaurus,* it had two long horns over its eyes and a shorter horn on its nose. But it also had a hornlike point on each cheek. *Pentaceratops* was a little more than 17 feet (5.2 m) long, and lived in what is now New Mexico.

Like the short-frilled ceratopsids, the long-frills lived in huge herds and roamed the countryside. They were among the last dinosaurs of the Age of Dinosaurs. One of the very last kind of dinosaurs to become extinct was *Torosaurus.*

When a Torosaurus lowered its head, its huge frill lifted up. This made the Torosaurus look much bigger and might frighten off an attacker.

pentaceratopses

Pachycephalosaurus

(pak uh SEHF uh loh sawr uhs)

A small group of dinosaurs stood on a hillside, feeding on the leaves of a cluster of trees. The dinosaurs moved on two legs, body bent forward and tail sticking straight out. Their heads were oddly shaped, with big rounded bumps on top.

Two of the animals had stopped eating and stood

a distance apart, facing each other. They were males, slightly larger than most of the others in the herd.

Suddenly, one of the males lowered his head and charged straight at the other! In an instant, the second male had put his head down and bounded forward. The two met at full speed, their heads knocking together with a *crack* that shook the air!

The force of the blow made each of them

stagger back a few steps. But neither was hurt. They eyed each other again for a moment, then one turned away and began to munch on leaves on a nearby tree.

We call this dinosaur *Pachycephalosaurus*, which means "thick-headed lizard." Of course, it got the name from the dome of bone, 10 inches (25 centimeters) thick, on the top of the head. Besides this dome, it also had clusters of bony knobs on the back of its head and clusters of short, bony spikes on its snout.

Why would an animal have such a dome on its head? Most scientists think these dinosaurs acted much like many kinds of goats do today—the males may have fought each other, at mating time, by banging their heads together. The thick dome would have kept them from getting hurt. But after butting their heads together a few times, one of them would give up and the other would win the female for a mate.

However, it is also possible that these dinosaurs used their thick, bony bumps as weapons, to fight off big meat-eating carnosaurs. Several large male pachycephalosauruses might have teamed up to charge a meat-eating enemy, slamming headfirst into its ribs and hips. They might have been able to injure even a big *Tyrannosaurus*.

Pachycephalosauruses apparently roamed the hills and mountainsides in what is now western North America. They were about 15 feet (4.6 meters) long, and probably walked on two legs all

of the time. They were not fast runners, but they had sharp eyes and a good sense of smell to warn them of approaching carnosaurs. They ate leaves, fruits, seeds, and, perhaps, insects.

A number of different kinds of dome-headed dinosaurs, much like *Pachycephalosaurus* only smaller, lived in North America and Asia during the last part of the Cretaceous Period. *Stegoceras* (stehg uh SEHR uhs), meaning "roof horn," was about 6½ feet (2 m) long. It had a high, round dome and a ring of knobs around the back of its head. Its snout was much shorter than the snout of *Pachycephalosaurus*. However, *Stegoceras* may have been the ancestor of *Pachycephalosaurus*.

The smallest dome-head was a dinosaur named *Micropachycephalosaurus* (my kroh pak uh SEHF uh luh SAWR uhs), meaning "tiny thick-headed lizard." It was only about 20 inches (51 cm) long and lived in China.

Micropachycephalosaurus

Troödon
(TROH uh dahn)

One of the first dinosaur fossils found in the
United States, more than 130 years ago, was a
tooth. It was a rather small tooth, shaped like a
triangle. It had a sharp point and sawlike edges.
Such a tooth looked as if it could bite deeply into
flesh, so the dinosaur from which the tooth had
come was given the name *Troödon,* meaning
"wounding tooth." A great many years went by
and only one other *Troödon* fossil was found—a
piece of jaw. Scientists still didn't have enough
information to be able to tell what kind of dinosaur
Troödon was. Because of its sharp tooth, some
scientists felt sure it was a meat-eater. That would

237

have made it a theropod, or "beast foot," like all meat-eating dinosaurs. But other scientists thought it might have been some kind of bone-headed dinosaur, like *Pachycephalosaurus*. If so, it would have been an ornithopod, or "bird foot." And all ornithopods were plant-eaters, so far as was known at that time.

Then, in 1980, two scientists found a great many *Troödon* fossils in one place. There were more teeth, a jaw, a thighbone and other bones, and even some eggs and skeletons of baby troödons. From all these fossils, scientists were able to tell what kind of dinosaur *Troödon* had been. And what they found out astounded them.

Troödon turned out to be an ornithopod, but it was also obviously a meat-eater. This was amazing, because every other meat-eating dinosaur known was a theropod. And every other ornithopod ever discovered was a plant-eater. Sharp-toothed little *Troödon* was the only meat-eating ornithopod. It was as if scientists had discovered a cow that ate rabbits!

Troödons were small hunters, about 8 feet (2.4 meters) long. They probably looked very much like the harmless plant-eater *Hypsilophodon*—except for their sharp teeth! They lived in what is now the state of Montana and part of Alberta, Canada, about 70 million years ago.

Segnosaurus
(sehg nuh SAWR uhs)

Not very much is known about the dinosaur named *Segnosaurus*, or "slow lizard." But what is known makes it seem rather puzzling.

A *Segnosaurus* probably walked on four legs. It was about 30 feet (9 meters) long and 8 feet (2.4 m) high. These animals were saurischians, or lizard-hipped dinosaurs, like all the meat-eaters such as *Tyrannosaurus* and *Deinonychus*. Segnosauruses were surely meat-eaters, too, for they had rows of small sharp teeth, and long, sharp claws on their four-toed feet.

But, in some ways, a *Segnosaurus* was much like an ornithischian, or bird-hipped plant-eater such as *Iguanodon* or *Triceratops*. Its hipbones were much more birdlike than lizardlike, and the front part of its jaws ended in a birdlike beak, such

as many plant-eaters had. The plant-eaters used their beaks to snip off tough stems and leaves, so it is puzzling that a meat-eater had such a beak.

However, some scientists think that *Segnosaurus* may have used its beak for catching fish. Segnosauruses may have been swimming dinosaurs that spent most of their time in water and lived on fish!

A good reason for thinking so is that some fossil footprints of webbed feet with four toes, such as segnosauruses had, were found near *Segnosaurus* bones. Animals with webbed feet are water animals, so if these are *Segnosaurus* footprints, which seems likely, segnosauruses must have been water animals.

Segnosauruses lived in what is now Mongolia, in Asia.

Avimimus

(ay vih MY muhs)

Avimimus was a little dinosaur that may have looked very much like a bird. That is why it was given its name, which means "bird imitator." It apparently had short, broad wings, a long, feathered tail, and birdlike legs and feet. But it probably had a lizardlike head with teeth in the jaws.

Although these little dinosaurs had wings, they couldn't fly. At the most, they could probably just flutter up into the air for a few moments, perhaps to snap at a flying insect. But they were fast runners that darted about after insects and little lizards, and perhaps small, furry animals.

An *Avimimus* had big eyes and a big brain for its size. So it may have been fairly smart. And it may have been able to see well in dim light such as twilight or moonlight. These birdlike dinosaurs lived in what is now Mongolia, probably on plains or perhaps in deserts. They were from 3 to 5 feet (1–1.5 meters) long.

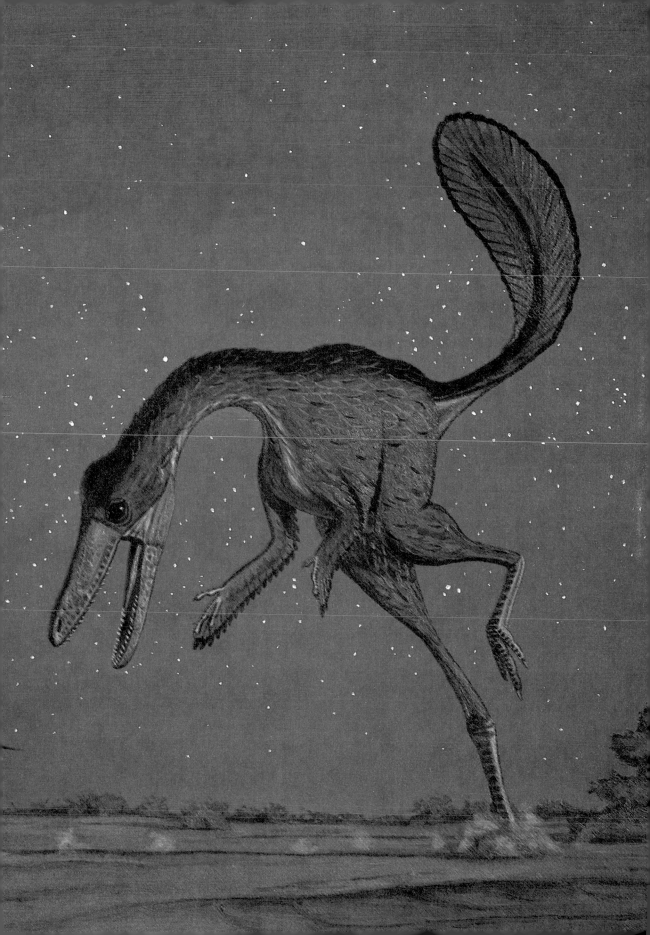

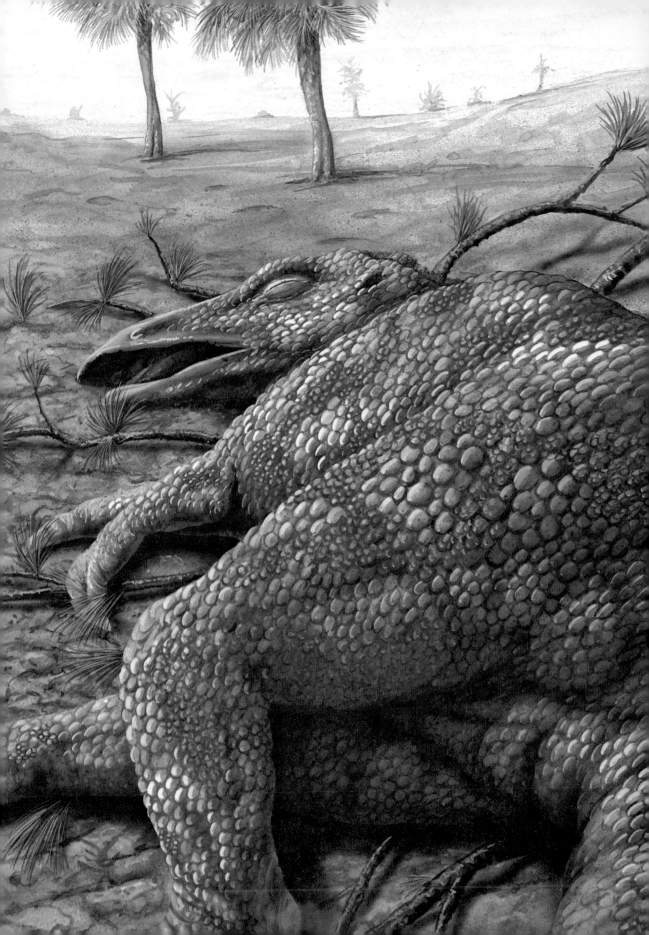

Anatosaurus

(uh nat uh SAWR uhs)

The dinosaur was dying. Unable to walk, it had fallen to the ground. It lay, breathing weakly, not understanding what was happening to it. After a time, it stopped breathing.

Most of the time when a dinosaur died, other creatures soon found its body and fed on its flesh and skin. The parts not eaten would rot away. After a time, only bones would be left. But that did not happen to this dead dinosaur. No other creatures found it, and it lay beneath the hot sun, day after day. Instead of rotting, the body began to dry out. The skin shrank until it stretched tightly over the bones. The dinosaur became a mummy—a dried-out dead body.

In time, wind-blown sand covered the mummy. This helped keep it dry and protected. As more time went on, it was buried more and more deeply. As millions of years went by, it became fossilized, with both its bones and its dried skin turning to stone. Early in the 1900's, this fossilized dinosaur mummy was discovered and dug up.

The dinosaur was a two-legged plant-eater. It had jaws that formed a bill, like the bill of a duck or goose. It was a dinosaur that scientists already knew something about. A number of skeletons and bones of this kind of dinosaur had been found

before the fossilized mummy was discovered. It had been named *Anatosaurus*, or "duck lizard," because of its ducklike bill.

But the mummy provided information that plain bones could not give. It showed that an *Anatosaurus*'s skin was much like the skin of the present-day lizard called a Gila (HEE luh) monster. It was covered with tiny bumps and dotted here and there with clusters of bigger bumps. The *Anatosaurus*'s four-fingered hands were webbed, like the feet of a duck or other water animal. And a kind of ruffle of thick skin ran down its neck, back, and tail.

The mummy also showed exactly what an *Anatosaurus* ate. The *Anatosaurus* must have eaten shortly before it died, for there was undigested food in its stomach. The food had been dried out and fossilized along with the animal. It consisted of pine tree needles, twigs, fruits, and seeds.

And so, a great deal is known about this kind of dinosaur and others like it. It was one of the duckbilled dinosaurs. This large group of dinosaurs all have the name hadrosaur (HAD ruh sawr), meaning "stout lizard." The hadrosaurs were descended from dinosaurs like *Iguanodon* and were one of the most common kind of dinosaurs.

Anatosaurus and other hadrosaurs spent most of their time on land, but were probably very good swimmers. They moved about on two legs to munch needles off pine trees, and probably got down on all fours to browse on low-growing plants. They had no teeth in their bill, but they had as many as two thousand teeth farther back in their jaws. Instead of just being in rows around the jaws, as our teeth are, a hadrosaur had masses of teeth that formed one solid, packed-together "pavement" on each side of its mouth. It could easily grind such things as pine needles and twigs to a soft pulp. And as its teeth wore out from such hard chewing, new ones grew in to take their place.

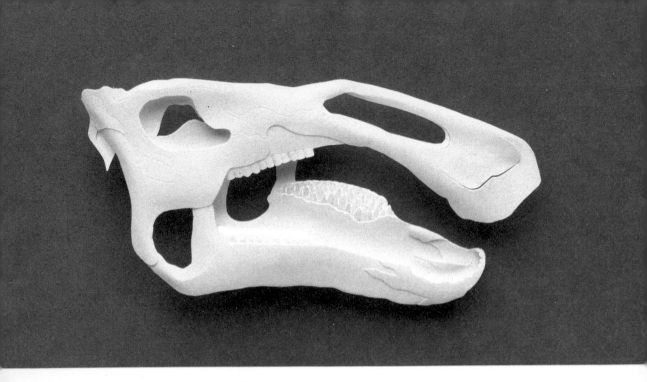

This model hadrosaur skull has part of the jaw cut
away to show how a hadrosaur's teeth were arranged.

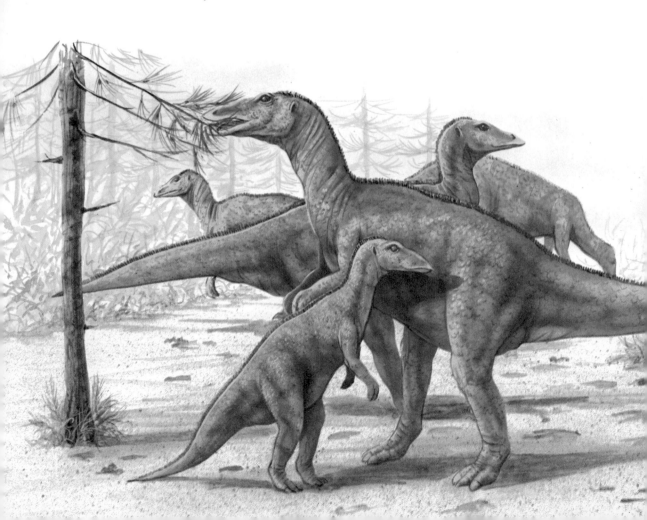

Scientists think that anatosauruses and other hadrosaurs lived in large herds. Living in a herd may have helped keep them safe from dangerous carnosaurs. They apparently took good care of their young, in much the same way many birds do today. When the herd went searching for food, the young were kept in the middle of the herd. Surrounded in this way, they were protected by the adults.

Many kinds of hadrosaurs, much like *Anatosaurus*, lived in almost all parts of the world. The biggest of them, *Shantungosaurus* (shan tuhng uh SAWR uhs), found in Shantung, China, was 49 feet (15 meters) long. *Anatosaurus* was about 33 feet (10 m) long, and lived in what are now the states of Wyoming and Montana, and in Alberta, Canada. It lived near the end of the Cretaceous Period, and was one of the last kind of dinosaurs.

Maiasaura
(my uh SAWR uh)

On a broad, flat area of ground not far from a river, a number of female hadrosaurs had made nests. They had pushed mud together to form small mounds about 10 feet (3 meters) wide and 5 feet (1.5 m) high. In the top of her mound, each female had scooped out a shallow pit. In this pit she had laid from twenty to twenty-five eggs.

Many of the hadrosaurs were crouched in their pits. They were keeping the eggs warm with their bodies so that the eggs would hatch. But in some

of the nests the eggs had already hatched. Clusters of feeble, helpless baby hadrosaurs squirmed and wriggled in the bottom of the pits. Their mothers had left to search for food.

Even though the babies were left alone, they were quite safe. The nests were no farther apart than the length of a female hadrosaur's body—about 30 feet (9 m). With so many of the mother hadrosaurs lying in their nests, no small egg-stealing or meat-eating dinosaur would dare come among them to try to snatch up a baby. Perhaps not even a big carnosaur would be willing to face so many enemies. And so, the young ones were well protected.

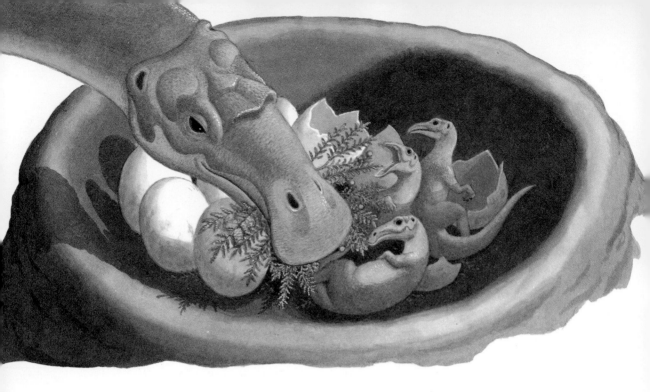

In time, one of the mothers returned. In her duckbilled jaws she carried a wad of pine tree branches, green with needles and thick with pine cones. She dropped this into the shallow pit. At once, the baby dinosaurs, each about a foot (30 centimeters) long, squirmed and waddled to this food and began to eat.

The name given these duckbilled hadrosaurs that made nests and took such good care of their young is *Maiasaura*, which means "good-mother lizard." Maiasauras looked much like anatosauruses, except that they had a short, bony spike sticking up between the eyes, and they were just a little smaller. Scientists know about how maiasauras cared for their young because a number of fossilized *Maiasaura* nests have been found, with both eggshells and skeletons of young maiasauras in them. This shows that young maiasauras stayed in the nest for a time after they hatched. Their mothers must have fed them, just as many mother birds of today feed their young ones in the nest.

Young maiasauras probably stayed in the nest until they were big enough to walk well. Then they may have stayed close to their mother for a time, learning where and how to find their own food and how to look after themselves. Finally, they would have been big enough to join the rest of the herd of adults.

Maiasauras lived in what is now the state of Montana.

Corythosaurus

Lambeosaurus

Hadrosaurs with head ornaments

(HAD ruh sawrz)

Maiasaura, Anatosaurus, and a few other kinds of duckbilled hadrosaurs are what are known as "flat-headed" hadrosaurs. This is because many other kinds of hadrosaurs had "ornaments" on their heads—crests, spikes, and tubes.

The hadrosaur called *Corythosaurus* (kuh rihth uh SAWR uhs) had a thin half-circle of bone, like the crest of an ancient helmet, across the top of its skull. This crest gives *Corythosaurus* its name, which means "helmet lizard." Apparently, male corythosauruses had large crests, while the females and young had smaller ones.

A male *Lambeosaurus* (lam bee uh SAWR uhs) had a hatchet-shaped crest sticking up from its skull. A blunt spike stuck up at the back of the crest. However, perhaps skin covered or hung from the crest and spike when these animals were alive. This might have made the "ornaments" look very different. Female and young lambeosauruses had smaller, somewhat differently shaped crests. *Lambeosaurus,* which means "Lambe's lizard," was named after Lawrence Lambe, the scientist who discovered it.

The skull of a *Parasaurolophus* (par uh sawr AWL uh fuhs) has a curved tube 6 feet (1.8 meters)

The hadrosaur called *Parasaurolphus* may or may
not have had a flap of skin hanging from the long
tube that stuck out of the back of its head.

long sticking out of the back of it. Perhaps when
the animal was alive a flap of skin hung from the
tube to *Parasaurolophus*'s neck. *Parasaurolophus*
means "like the lizard with a crest."

Tsintaosaurus (chin TAY uh sawr uhs), or
"Tsintao lizard," is named for the city in China
where it was found. It had a long, spiky horn
between its eyes. There may have been a skin flap
attached to this when the animal was alive.

There were a number of other hadrosaurs with
similar crests, horns, and spikes. The problem is,
what were all these head ornaments for? Usually,
every part of an animal's body has some purpose.

What was the purpose of these strange things on a hadrosaur's head?

Scientists have several ideas. One is that the ornaments may have helped give these dinosaurs a better sense of smell. In most of the crests and tubes, long air passages connected with the animal's nose. This may have had the effect of making the smelling part of a hadrosaur's nose much longer, so that it would have been able to pick up even the faintest odors. This could have been a big help if there were a carnosaur in the distance, because by smelling it early the hadrosaur could run away before it got closer.

Another idea is that hadrosaurs' head ornaments were "noisemakers." If hadrosaurs roared or bellowed or squawked or honked, the sound would have gone through the air passages and been made louder, like sound going through a trumpet. Perhaps hadrosaurs made loud, trumpeting sounds to call to each other at mating time, or to warn one another when danger was near.

There is evidence that even the flat-headed hadrosaurs had a way of making their voices louder. From the way their skulls are formed, it looks as if they may have had loose flaps of skin on their snouts, which they could blow up like a balloon. This would have worked the same way as the air passages in a crest or tube, and made a bellow or squawk sound louder.

Corythosaurus

Lambeosaurus

Parasaurolophus

These model skulls show the air passages in the crests of three different kinds of hadrosaurs.

Head ornaments, such as the one on this mother Tsintaosaurus, may have helped baby hadrosaurs recognize their parents.

Still another idea is that the ornaments on hadrosaurs' heads were simply a way for hadrosaurs of the same kind to recognize one another at mating time. There were many different kinds of hadrosaurs. Without head ornaments, they probably would have all looked pretty much alike. But a hadrosaur seeing another animal with a head ornament like its own, would have been attracted to it. Some scientists think the head ornaments might even have been brightly colored at mating time, as parts of the bodies of some birds are today.

Corythosaurus, *Parasaurolophus*, and *Lambeosaurus* all lived in what is now western Canada and some of the western states of the United States. Fossils of other hadrosaurs with head ornaments have been found in China, Mongolia, and Japan.

Tyrannosaurus

(tih ran uh SAWR uhs)

Seventy million years ago, a gigantic and dreadful-looking creature prowled about in what is now western North America. It was some 40 feet (12 meters) long and stood 18½ feet (5.6 m) high. It had jaws three feet (1 m) long that were ringed with teeth 7¼ inches (18.4 centimeters) long. The teeth were saw-edged and like pointed daggers. On its toes, it had great curved claws. It was the largest meat-eating animal that has ever lived on land. This monstrous carnosaur has been named *Tyrannosaurus*, meaning "tyrant lizard."

A tyrant is a cruel, merciless ruler, and *Tyrannosaurus* got its name because scientists thought such a huge, frightful beast must have been a kind of tyrant. They felt it probably ruled its area much as a lion or tiger does today, striking fear into all other animals and killing whatever and whenever it wished.

Tyrannosauruses ate flesh, of course, but what kind of flesh? Hadrosaurs—duckbilled dinosaurs—were numerous in the places where tyrannosauruses lived. They were slow-moving and defenseless, and they may have been a *Tyrannosaurus*'s main prey. Herds of horned dinosaurs such as *Triceratops* also roamed the land in which tyrannosauruses hunted. But a

Tyrannosaurus probably wouldn't have tried to charge into a herd of horned dinosaurs to attack one. More likely, it would have just stayed near the herd, watching for a young one to stray away from the others.

How did a *Tyrannosaurus* hunt? Some scientists think these big animals could run very fast for short distances. A *Tyrannosaurus* might have waited in hiding for a hadrosaur or other dinosaur to get close, and then made a quick rush. It would have seized its prey in its huge jaws, and used the claws on its feet to slash and tear the other animal's body.

However, many scientists do not think tyrannosauruses were hunters at all. They think, from the way the animal's hipbones are formed, that a *Tyrannosaurus* could not even move as fast as a person can walk. They think tyrannosauruses probably just plodded about, looking for the bodies of dead dinosaurs to eat. In other words, tyrannosauruses may have been much like vultures, hyenas, and some other animals of today that eat carrion (KAR ee uhn). Carrion is dead, decaying meat. Animals that feed on the bodies of dead animals are called carrion eaters.

However a *Tyrannosaurus* got its food, it was certainly able to eat it easily. With its powerful jaws and sharp, shearing teeth it could rip off huge chunks of meat and swallow them whole.

A *Tyrannosaurus*'s arms were tiny for its huge size and apparently useless. The hands had only two fingers tipped with tiny claws. A *Tyrannosaurus* couldn't have used such tiny arms and hands to hold its prey, or to fight with. So what were they good for? Although they were small, the arms were strong. Scientists think a *Tyrannosaurus* used them to push itself up after it had been lying down to sleep, rest, or eat.

Tyrannosauruses were only one kind of a large group of animals that were very much alike. They are all known as tyrannosaurids (tih ran uh SAWR ihds). One of these creatures, *Albertosaurus* (al bur tuh SAWR uhs), or "Alberta lizard," lived in what is now Alberta, Canada. It was a little smaller than *Tyrannosaurus*, but had more teeth. *Tarbosaurus* (TAHR buh sawr uhs), which means "fearsome lizard," lived in Mongolia. Some tarbosauruses were even bigger than a *Tyrannosaurus*!

Therizinosaurus

(thehr ihz IHN uh sawr uhs)

Very little is known about the dinosaur named *Therizinosaurus,* or "scythe lizard." But from what is known of it, some scientists think it may have been the most ferocious and terrible of all the meat-eating dinosaurs!

All that has been found of *Therizinosaurus* is part of a leg, a tooth, the bone of one arm, and a clawed hand. But what an arm and hand! The arm is more than 8 feet (2.4 meters) long. And the hand is tipped with enormous, sharp claws, curved like the farm tool called a scythe—which is why this dinosaur was given the name it has.

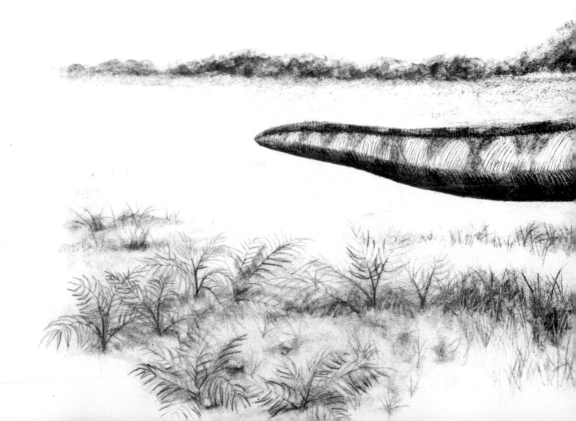

With such claws, it seems as if a *Therizinosaurus* could have killed duckbilled dinosaurs, and perhaps even armored dinosaurs, as easily as a lion kills an antelope. However, this dinosaur may have used its huge, curved claws in other ways. Perhaps it used them for tearing something open, as an anteater uses its claws to tear open an anthill.

There's no way of telling exactly how big a *Therizinosaurus* was, but it may have been 35 feet (10.7 m) long, and maybe much more! These dinosaurs lived in what is now Mongolia.

Saurornithoides
(sawr awr nuh THOY deez)

Near the end of the Cretaceous Period, in what is now Mongolia, there lived big-eyed, two-legged, meat-eating dinosaurs that were probably the smartest of all dinosaurs—and may have been the smartest of all reptiles that have ever lived! They have been named *Saurornithoides*, meaning "birdlike lizard," because they had light, slim, birdlike bodies. A *Saurornithoides* was about 6 feet (1.8 meters) long.

Like the small meat-eating dinosaur *Deinonychus*, a *Saurornithoides* had a stiff tail and a sharp, curved claw that stuck up on each foot. These dinosaurs probably hunted mostly small creatures such as lizards and mammals. They ran very swiftly, with stiff tails stretched straight out. They used their three-fingered hands to snatch up prey. Because a *Saurornithoides* had very large eyes, most scientists think these dinosaurs must have done their hunting at dusk or night, when many of the little mammals would have come out of hiding.

Dinosaurs much like *Saurornithoides* lived in what is now Alberta, Canada. For their size, all these dinosaurs had a very large brain, and may have been much smarter than any other kind of reptile. Some scientists think that if dinosaurs hadn't become extinct, descendants of dinosaurs like *Saurornithoides* might have become as intelligent as people!

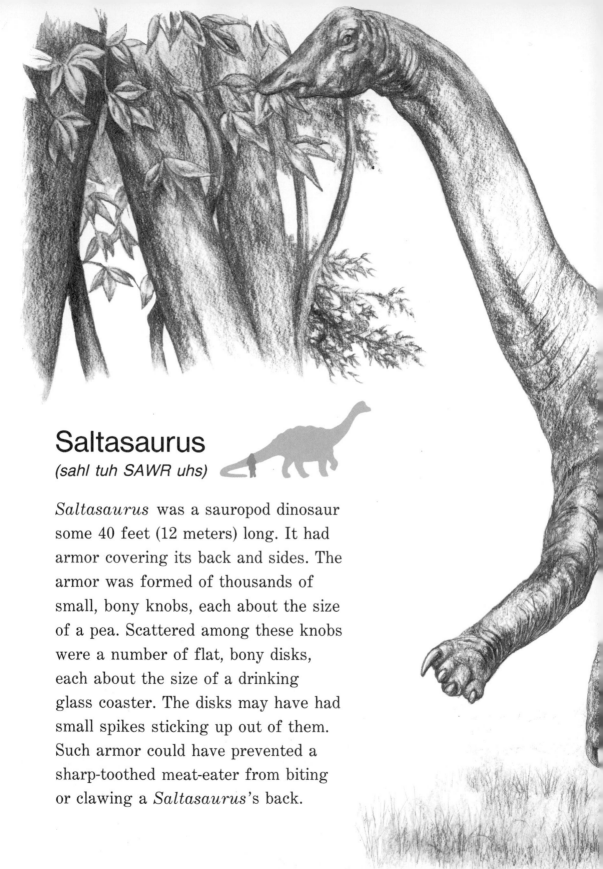

Saltasaurus
(sahl tuh SAWR uhs)

Saltasaurus was a sauropod dinosaur some 40 feet (12 meters) long. It had armor covering its back and sides. The armor was formed of thousands of small, bony knobs, each about the size of a pea. Scattered among these knobs were a number of flat, bony disks, each about the size of a drinking glass coaster. The disks may have had small spikes sticking up out of them. Such armor could have prevented a sharp-toothed meat-eater from biting or clawing a *Saltasaurus*'s back.

A *Saltasaurus* had very broad, strong bones in the upper part of its tail. This causes scientists to think that it could probably rear up on its back legs, using its tail for support, in order to reach bunches of leaves high up on trees. These dinosaurs lived about 70 million years ago in what is now the country of Argentina. They are named for the place where their fossil bones were found, the province of Salta, Argentina.

Thescelosaurus
(thehs kehl uh SAWR uhs)

One of the last kind of dinosaurs was a two-legged plant-eater named *Thescelosaurus,* or "wonderful lizard." It lived at the very end of the Cretaceous Period.

 A *Thescelosaurus* was 11 feet (3.4

meters) long, or about as long as a small car. It had a long, low body and a stiff tail that stuck straight out. It was an ornithopod, or bird-footed dinosaur. Like most ornithopods, it had cheeks. But unlike most ornithopods, it was apparently partly armored, because there were rows of bony knobs along its back.

Thescelosauruses lived in what is now Alberta and Saskatchewan, in Canada, and Wyoming and Montana, in the United States.

Ichthyornis

Hesperornis

Other animals of the Cretaceous Period

Birds probably first appeared in the Triassic Period. They apparently increased and spread out greatly during the Cretaceous Period. There were a number of different kinds by the end of the period.

One of these looked very much like a sea gull, except that it had small, curved teeth in its bill. It could probably fly as well as any bird of today. It lived along seacoasts, in what is now North America, and preyed on fish, just as gulls now do. It has been named *Ichthyornis* (ihk thee AWR nihs), or "fish bird."

A very different sort of bird was *Hesperornis* (hehs puh RAWR nihs), or "western bird." It had a body 5 feet (1.5 meters) long and tiny, useless wings. It was a swimmer and diver and swam by paddling with its big, webbed feet. It, too, lived along ancient North American seacoasts, where it dived and swam after fish. Its long, pointed beak was filled with sharp teeth.

The pterosaurs, or flying reptiles, also did well throughout the Cretaceous Period. Some kinds became far bigger than any of the Jurassic pterosaurs.

Pteranodon (tehr AN uh dahn), or "winged without teeth," was a pterosaur about the size of a goose. But it had wings that stretched 26 feet (8 m) from tip to tip. Pteranodons lived along seashores in what is now Kansas, Texas, Delaware,

pteranodons

and Japan. They probably lived mainly on fish, which they snapped up with their long, toothless beaks as they skimmed over the water. They may have had throat pouches, as modern pelicans do, in which they could hold fish to take to their young ones.

The biggest flying creature that has ever lived was a Cretaceous pterosaur that has been found in North America, Africa, and the Middle East. It had a body nearly 6 feet (1.8 m) long, and wings that stretched to 39 feet (12 m). It probably flew much as a condor or albatross does today, gliding on currents of air. It may have lived much as vultures now do, soaring high in the sky, peering down in search of the bodies of dead dinosaurs it could glide down to and eat. This giant flying reptile has been named *Quetzalcoatlus* (keht sahl koh AH tuhl uhs), or "feathered serpent," after an ancient Aztec god.

The gigantic Cretaceous pterosaur *Quetzalcoatlus* probably fed on the bodies of dead dinosaurs.

Crocodiles, too, did well during the Cretaceous Period. Some kinds were as fierce and terrifying as the biggest meat-eating dinosaurs! *Deinosuchus* (dy nuh SOOK uhs), or "terrible crocodile," which lived in what is now Texas, was probably more than 50 feet (15 m) long—longer than *Tyrannosaurus*. These giant crocodiles probably lurked in rivers, near the banks, to prey on small and medium-sized dinosaurs that came to drink.

The Cretaceous seas still abounded with ichthyosaurs and long-necked and short-necked plesiosaurs. *Elasmosaurus* (ih laz muh SAWR uhs), or "metal plate lizard," was a long-necked plesiosaur. It had a body 40 feet (12 m) long—but the neck and head made up half of that length.

Kronosaurus (krohn uh SAWR uhs) was a gigantic short-necked plesiosaur that was 56 feet (17 m) long including its huge head, which was 9 feet (2.7 m) long. *Kronosaurus* is named for the god Cronus, or Kronos, in Greek mythology. *Elasmosaurus* lived in seas covering parts of North America, and *Kronosaurus* lived in seas that washed over what is now Australia.

Elasmosaurus

mosasaur

A giant new creature also appeared in the
Cretaceous seas near the end of the period. It was
an enormous sea-dwelling lizard with a long,
fishlike body and four big paddles. These creatures
are known as mosasaurs (MOH suh sawrz), or
"Meuse lizards," because the first fossil of one
was found near the Meuse River in Europe. The
biggest were about 30 feet (9 m) long. They ate

archelons

fish and ammonites (AM uh nyts). Ammonites were shellfish somewhat like a squid. They had a coiled shell that was up to 6 feet (1.8 m) across.

Giant sea turtles were common in the late part of the Cretaceous Period. One of these, *Archelon* (AHR kuh lahn), meaning "king turtle," was the largest turtle that has ever lived. It was 12 feet (3.6 m) long and 11 feet (3.3 m) wide. It lived in the great sea that covered much of North America seventy million years ago.

A brand new kind of creature appeared on the land during the Cretaceous Period. It was a lizardlike reptile with a long, slim, legless body—the snake. Some of the larger snakes of the Cretaceous Period were about 6 feet (1.8 m) long.

New kinds of mammals also appeared in the last part of the Cretaceous Period. One was a mammal that was like a kind still around today—the common opossum (uh PAHS uhm). The name comes from an American Indian word meaning "white animal." Like the opossum of today, the largest Cretaceous opossum was about 40 inches (1 m) long, including the tail. It may have had a long pointed nose, five-toed paws, and a long, skinny tail. Females had pouches, like kangaroos, in which they carried their babies for about two weeks. Then the babies, usually around ten in number, would ride on their mother's back for a time.

Cretaceous opossums probably ate insects, lizards, seeds, roots, and dinosaur eggs when they could. Like modern opossums, they probably stayed hidden by day and came out at night.

What happened to the dinosaurs?

The Cretaceous Period ended about 65 million years ago. During the last hundred thousand years or so of the Cretaceous, a great many things were happening. There were many volcanic eruptions. New mountain ranges, such as the American Rockies, began to form. The continents began to lift up and the sea level started to drop. The climate started to grow cooler.

All during the Cretaceous Period, stretches of mud, sand, and ooze hardened into layers of rock that make up part of the earth's surface today. Dinosaurs that lived and died in that mud, sand,

and ooze left fossils in the rock—bones, skeletons, footprints, eggs. Some of these fossils are found near the top of the Cretaceous rock—the last layer to be formed before the period ended.

But there do not seem to be any dinosaur fossils in the next layer of rock, which was formed at the beginning of the period right after the Cretaceous. What this means is that dinosaurs apparently died out at the end of the Cretaceous Period. It seems that none of them survived into the next period, or there would be dinosaur fossils in that rock.

Dinosaurs are not the only animals that seem to have died out at the end of the Cretaceous Period. There are no fossils of ichthyosaurs, plesiosaurs, mosasaurs, pterosaurs, or several other kinds of animals in the later rock, either.

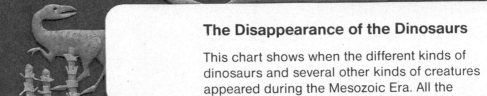

The Disappearance of the Dinosaurs

This chart shows when the different kinds of dinosaurs and several other kinds of creatures appeared during the Mesozoic Era. All the

Mesozoic Era

Triassic Period
245-208 million years ago

Jurassic Period
208-144 million years ago

prosauropods

sauropods

coelurosaurs

carnosaurs

stegosaurs

ornithopods

ankylosaurs

lizards

birds

mammals

crocodilians

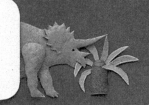

dinosaurs apparently became extinct at the end of the era, but birds, mammals, and other animals continued on to the present day. What happened to the dinosaurs is one of the greatest scientific mysteries.

Cenozoic Era

Cretaceous Period
144-65 million years ago

65 million years ago to the present day

ceratopsians

snakes

This is one of the biggest mysteries that scientists have puzzled over. The dinosaurs and several other kinds of creatures apparently died out at the end of the Cretaceous Period. But why? Many kinds of creatures did live on past the end of the Cretaceous, of course—birds, mammals, and a number of kinds of reptiles. But what caused a smart, fast creature like the dinosaur *Saurornithoides* to become extinct, while big, slow, rather stupid crocodiles survived? Why did the winged pterosaurs apparently die out, while winged birds multiplied? What happened?

There are two main ideas.

Some scientists have found evidence that something unusual happened just as the Cretaceous Period was ending. They think a huge meteorite, or chunk of rock from space, smashed into the earth and caused the death of all the dinosaurs!

There are many such chunks of rock, which we call meteoroids, moving in space. Sometimes, one of them will come near enough to the earth so that earth's gravity gets hold of it and begins to pull it down. In most cases, the meteoroid is burned up by friction as it rushes down through earth's atmosphere. It becomes what we call a meteor, or "shooting star." But if it is big enough, it may not burn up completely. If enough of it is left to hit the ground, we call it a meteorite. If it is big enough when it smashes into the ground, it makes a large crater, or pit.

Scientists have found evidence that a really gigantic meteoroid streaked into earth's atmosphere near the end of the Cretaceous Period. It was traveling at a speed of about 60,000 miles (100,000 kilometers) per hour. It crashed into the earth with such force that it dug a crater some 120 miles (200 km) wide. The force with which it struck the earth must have hurled tons and tons of powdered rock and soil up into the air.

This powdered rock and soil would have spread out and formed a huge cloud in the atmosphere,

covering the entire planet. The cloud would have been so thick and dark that it would have blocked off much of the sunlight that usually reaches the earth. With almost no warm sunlight, the green plants, which need sunlight for life, would have begun to die. And the weather would have turned colder.

Soon, there would not have been enough food for plant-eating dinosaurs. Many would have died of starvation. As the plant-eaters became fewer and fewer, there would have been less food for meat-eating dinosaurs. They, too, would have died. And some dinosaurs might have died simply because of the colder weather. Thus, in time, the dinosaurs would have become extinct, for scientists think that the dark cloud may have stayed in the sky for at least three months.

However, other scientists doubt that things happened quite that way. While many agree that a giant meteorite may have struck the earth at the end of the Cretaceous Period, they don't think it had much to do with what happened to the dinosaurs.

For one thing, these scientists say that if the meteorite made things so bad that all the dinosaurs were wiped out, why weren't all other animals wiped out, too? How could crocodiles, many of which were as big as some dinosaurs, manage to survive when dinosaurs couldn't? How did many

birds, mammals, snakes, and lizards stay alive? These scientists think that conditions couldn't have been as bad as the other scientists believe, or else everything would have been wiped out.

They also say there is evidence that many kinds of dinosaurs had actually become extinct long before the meteorite struck. Furthermore, there seems to be evidence that some kinds of dinosaurs lived on, long after the time of the meteorite—as much as a million years after! Thus, it looks to these scientists as if the extinction of the dinosaurs took place slowly, over a long time.

So, as things stand right now, some scientists think that dinosaurs suddenly became extinct

because a huge meteorite struck the earth. Other scientists think the dinosaurs died out very slowly, because of the change in climate, the drying up of the seas, and all the other things that took place around the end of the Cretaceous Period. Still other scientists say that dinosaurs didn't really become extinct at all, because birds are actually a kind of dinosaur!

Thus, the mystery of what happened to the dinosaurs is still as much a mystery as ever.

Books to Read

There are a great many good books about dinosaurs and their world. A few are listed here. Your school or public library will have some of these, as well as others.

Ages 5 to 8

The ABC Dinosaur Book by Jill Kingdom (Childrens Press, 1982)
An introduction to dinosaurs from A to Z, for younger children.

Baby Dinosaurs by Helen Roney Sattler (Lothrop, Lee & Shepard, 1984)
A well-written, colorfully illustrated book that explains what is known and what is believed about the life of several kinds of baby dinosaurs, from the time they hatched until they were "teen-agers."

The Crocodiles Still Wait by Carol Carrick (Houghton Mifflin/Clarion, 1980)
The life of a female giant crocodile of the time of the dinosaurs—hunting, nest-making, and care of the young.

Digging Up Dinosaurs by Aliki (Crowell, 1981)
Cartoon-style pictures show how scientists find fossils, dig them up, and prepare them for display in museums.

Dinosaurs and Their Young by Russell Freedman (Holiday House, 1983)
This book tells of the discovery of a fossil nest of baby hadrosaurs and eggs, and of similar discoveries, and explains how such discoveries help us learn how some kinds of dinosaurs reared their young.

Dinosaurs Are Different by Aliki (Crowell, 1985)
The author shows and explains how dinosaurs are classified (placed in related groups) according to their differences from one another.

Dinosaur Story by Joanna Cole (Morrow, 1974)
Short, clear, read-aloud text describes dinosaurs and their world, and helps younger children understand the time scale involved from dinosaur days to now.

Patrick's Dinosaurs by Carol Carrick (Houghton Mifflin, 1983)
A picture-story about a boy who begins to imagine dinosaurs everywhere on the streets of the city in which he lives—even peeking into his window! The dinosaur illustrations will help familiarize younger children with a number of different kinds of dinosaurs.

The Smallest Dinosaurs by Seymour Simon (Crown, 1982)
The author presents seven of the smallest dinosaurs, some of which may be related to the birds of today, and tells about their ways of life.

Supersaurus by Francine Jacobs (Putnam, 1982)
This story of the discovery of one of the largest of all dinosaurs gives readers an inside look at the work of a paleontologist, as well as a good understanding of how fossils are formed.

Ages 9 to 12

A Closer Look at Prehistoric Reptiles by Beverly Halstead (Franklin Watts, 1978)
This book covers the origin of reptiles and reptile groups including the dinosaurs, and also provides information about methods of reconstructing fossil animals.

Dinosaurs by Jasper Dimond (Prentice-Hall, 1985)
A book that combines information with punch-out figures of dinosaurs for making a miniature museum.

Dinosaurs and People: Fossils, Facts, and Fantasies by Laurence Pringle (Harcourt, Brace, 1978)
A complete history of the discovery of dinosaurs and of fossil hunting around the world, from the earliest days to the present.

Dinosaurs, Asteroids, and Superstars: Why the Dinosaurs Disappeared by Franklyn M. Branley (T. Y. Crowell, 1982)
This book covers many of the different ideas about what caused the extinction of the dinosaurs—volcanic activity, meteorite collision, etc. The author draws no conclusions, but leaves it up to the reader to consider all the possibilities for himself or herself.

Dinosaurs in Your Backyard by William Mannetti (Atheneum, 1982)
An interesting and informative book that deals mainly with the new idea that birds may be descended from dinosaurs, and that birds may thus be "dinosaurs in your backyard."

The Illustrated Dinosaur Dictionary by Helen Roney Sattler (Lothrop, Lee & Shepard, 1983)
An illustrated, alphabetical listing of more than 300 dinosaurs, including information on their ways of life.

Monster Dinosaur by Daniel Cohen (Lippincott, 1983)
An exciting book about the study of paleontology from the early 1800's to today. It covers much of the new, speculative information about dinosaurs, including whether they were warm-blooded and why they became extinct.

The Monsters Who Died: a Mystery About Dinosaurs by Vicki Cobb (Coward-McCann, 1983)
This book offers clear and accurate information about how scientists can tell what dinosaurs looked like and how they lived, and about the ideas dealing with how they might have become extinct.

Prehistoric Monsters by Jean Phillipe Varin (Salem House, 1985)
Models and restorations of dinosaurs, photographed in natural surroundings, make startlingly realistic illustrations, accompanied by informative text.

Pterosaurs, The Flying Reptiles by Helen Roney Sattler (Lothrop, Lee & Shepard, 1985)
A look at all the kinds of flying reptiles that lived during the time of the dinosaurs.

Ranger Rick's Dinosaur Book (National Wildlife Federation, 1984)
Dinosaurs and creatures that lived among them are presented in many full-color pictures and exciting text.

New Words

Here are some of the words you have met in this book. Many of them may be new to you. All are useful words to know. Next to each word, you'll see how to say the word: amphibian (am FIHB ee uhn). The part in capital letters is said more loudly than the rest of the word. One or two sentences tell what the word means.

amphibian (am FIHB ee uhn)
   An amphibian is an animal that hatches out of a soft egg that has no shell, in water or very damp earth. It generally lives in water and breathes with gills, like a fish, while it is young. It can live on land and breathe with lungs when it is an adult. Frogs, toads, and newts are amphibians.

ancestor (AN sehs tuhr)
   An ancestor is a plant, animal, or person of long ago from which a plant, animal, or person of a much later time is descended. Your grandparents are your ancestors.

arthritis (ar THRY tihs)
   Arthritis is a disease that causes the joints of a body, such as knees and elbows, to swell up and become sore.

browse (browz)
   To browse is to feed on leaves or grass by nibbling a bit here and there.

carrion (KAR ee uhn)
   Carrion is dead and rotting flesh. Many kinds of birds and animals of today are carrion eaters, and some dinosaurs probably were, also.

climate (KLY miht)
   Climate is the kind of weather that a place has steadily, over a period of many thousands, or even millions, of years.

cluster (KLUHS tuhr)
   A cluster is a number of objects or creatures, of the same kind, grouped together.

continent (KAHN tuh nuhnt)
   A continent is a gigantic mass of land, such as North America or Africa. Today there are seven continents, but during most of the time of the dinosaurs all seven continents were joined together, forming one giant continent.

crest (krehst)
   A crest is a tuft of feathers or hair, or a flap of skin or growth of bone on the head of a bird or animal. A rooster's comb is a crest. Several kinds of duckbilled dinosaurs had crests.

descendant (dee SEHN duhnt)
   A descendant is a living thing born into a group of living things that all have the same ancestors. Brothers and sisters of the same family are descendants of their grandparents.

erosion (ih ROH zhuhn)
   Erosion is the slow wearing away of soil and rock, mainly by wind and rain, but also by glaciers.

evidence (EV uh duhns)
   Evidence is proof of something. *Allosaurus* teeth marks in the bones of an *Apatosaurus* are evidence that allosauruses ate apatosauruses.

extinct (eck STIHNGKT)
   Extinct means no longer existing. When all of one kind of plant or animal have died out and there can never be any more, they are extinct.

family (FAM uh lee)
   In science, a family is a group of many kinds of related animals or

plants. For example, all the kinds of cats in the world, from housecats to tigers, make up the cat family.

flexible (FLEHK suh buhl)
A thing that is flexible is bendable.

flourish (FLUHR ish)
To flourish is to grow and do well. Flowers flourish with plenty of rain and sunshine.

fossil (FAHS uhl)
A fossil is the preserved remains or traces of a living thing of long ago.

frill (frihl)
A frill is a kind of fringe of feathers, hair, skin, or bone around the neck of a bird or animal. Most of the horned dinosaurs had a frill of bone growing out of the back of the head.

genus (JEE nuhs)
A genus is a scientific grouping of related animals or plants that are all alike in some special way. For example, lions, tigers, leopards, and all other kinds of very large cats make up one genus of the cat family.

mammal (MAM uhl)
Mammals are the kinds of animals that are warm-blooded, born from their mother's body instead of hatching from an egg, and fed milk from their mother's body as babies. All mammals have some hair on their bodies. Cats, dogs, apes, elephants, seals, whales, and people are some of the many kinds of mammals.

meteor (MEE tee uhr)
A meteor is a chunk of stone or metal from space that enters Earth's atmosphere and burns up as it falls to the ground. Meteors are often called falling stars or shooting stars.

meteorite (MEE tee uh ryt)
A meteorite is a meteor that reaches the ground before burning up completely.

meteoroid (MEE tee uh royd)
A meteoroid is a chunk of rock or metal that moves through space in orbit around the sun.

mummify (MUHM uh fy)
To mummify is to preserve by drying. A mummified animal is a dead animal whose body has been dried out so that it did not rot away, thus preserving the skin as well as the bones.

nomad (NOH mad)
A nomad is a person or animal that wanders about from place to place in order to find food.

order (AWR duhr)
An order is a large scientific grouping of many kinds of animals or plants that are all alike in some way. Dinosaurs in the ornithischian order all had birdlike hipbones.

reptile (REHP tuhl)
Reptiles are cold-blooded, scaly-skinned animals that hatch out of hard-shell eggs that are laid on land. Lizards, snakes, turtles, tuataras, alligators, and crocodiles are reptiles.

species (SPEE sheez)
A species is a scientific grouping of animals that are all exactly the same kind. The "broad-headed" *Triceratops* was a species of *Triceratops*.

survive (suhr VYVE)
To survive is to manage to live on, through a time of danger or difficulty, outlasting others.

trillion (TRIHL yuhn)
A trillion is one thousand billions in the United States and Canada. In Great Britain, it is one million billions.

vegetation (vehj uh TAY shuhn)
Vegetation is plant life.

Illustration Acknowledgments

The publishers of *Childcraft* gratefully acknowledge the courtesy of the following photographers, agencies, and organizations for illustrations in this volume. When all the illustrations for a sequence of pages are from a single source, the inclusive page numbers are given. Credits should be read from left to right, top to bottom, on their respective pages. All illustrations are the exclusive property of the publishers of *Childcraft* unless names are marked with an asterisk (*).

Cover: Aristocrat and Standard Binding—George Suyeoka, Photo by Ralph Brunke
Heritage Binding—John Dawson; Peter Barrett; Jean Helmer; Stephen Czerkas, National History Museum of Los Angeles County*; George Suyeoka, photo by Ralph Brunke; Colin Newman; Jean Helmer; John Dawson; Robert Hynes
Discovery Binding—Roberta Polfus
  1–3:   George Suyeoka, photo by Ralph Brunke
  8–9:   George Suyeoka, photo by Ralph Brunke
 10–11:   Larry Frederick
 12–13:   British Museum (Natural History)*; Larry Frederick; ©Alan Clifton, Aspect Picture Library*
 14–15:   Larry Frederick
 16–17:   Colin Newman
 18–21:   Bill Miller, photo by Ralph Brunke
 22–23:   Patricia Wynne
 24–25:   Jim Channell
 26–27:   George Suyeoka, photo by Ralph Brunke
 28–29:   Bill Miller, photo by Ralph Brunke
 30–31:   ©Mike Andrews, Earth Scenes*; Patricia Wynne
 32–33:   British Museum (Natural History)*; Institut Royal des Sciences Naturelles de Belgique*; John Fischner*
 34–35:   No. 3280, American Museum of Natural History*; Jim Channell
 36–37:   Jim Channell; ©Chip Clark*
 38–39:   Patricia Wynne; No. 324393, American Museum of Natural History*
 40–41:   Jim Pearson
 42–43:   No. 330491, American Museum of Natural History*
 44–45:   No. 35608, American Museum of Natural History*; Roberta Polfus
 46–47:   Jim Pearson; University of Nebraska*
 48–49:   Jim Pearson
 50–51:   Ghost Ranch Conference Center*; Bill Miller, photo by Ralph Brunke
 52–53:   ©Steve Leonard*
 54–55:   George Suyeoka, photo by Ralph Brunke
 56–59:   Peter Barrett
 60–61:   Jean Helmer
 62–63:   John Francis
 64–65:   Jennifer Emry-Perrott
 66–69:   Jean Helmer
 70–71:   Peter Barrett
 72–73:   Dr. Jose Bonaparte*; Jean Helmer
 74–75:   John Francis
 76–77:   No 322012, American Museum of Natural History*
 78–81:   Jean Helmer
 82–83:   John Francis
 84–85:   Peter Barrett
 86–87:   Jim Channell
 88–89:   Jennifer Emry-Perrott
 90–91:   Peter Barrett
 92–93:   Jennifer Emry-Perrott
 94–95:   George Suyeoka, photo by Ralph Brunke
 96–97:   Peter Barrett; Bill Miller, photo by Ralph Brunke
 98–99:   Peter Barrett
100–101:   Tom Leonard
102–103:   Jennifer Emry-Perrott
104–107:   Tom Leonard
108–109:   Jennifer Emry-Perrott
110–111:   Roberta Polfus
112–113:   Bill Miller, photo by Ralph Brunke; Stephen Czerkas, Natural History Museum of Los Angeles County*
114–115:   John Dawson
116–117:   Gregory Paul
118–121:   Roberta Polfus
122–123:   ©Steve Leonard*; Gregory Paul
124–125:   John Dawson
126–127:   No. 35422, American Museum of Natural History*
128–129:   John Dawson
130–131:   Edward Brooks
132–133:   John Dawson
134–135:   Edward Brooks
136–139:   John Dawson
140–141:   Museum fur Naturkunde, East Berlin*
142–143:   Jean Helmer
144–145:   ©Mark A. Philbrick*
146–147:   Roberta Polfus
148–151:   Phil Weare
152–153:   Dick Twinney
154–155:   Roberta Polfus
156–157:   Dick Twinney
158–159:   George Suyeoka, photo by Ralph Brunke
160–161:   Peter Barrett; Bill Miller, photo by Ralph Brunke
162–163:   Peter Barrett
164–165:   Peter Barrett; Roberta Polfus
166–167:   Roberta Polfus
168–175:   Jean Helmer
176–177:   Phil Weare
178–181:   Edward Brooks
182–183:   Phil Weare
184–187:   Edward Brooks
188–191:   Phil Weare
192–195:   Jim Pearson
196–197:   Samantha Carol Smith
198–201:   Robert Hynes
202–203:   Samantha Carol Smith
204–205:   John Francis
206–207:   Colin Newman
208–209:   Samantha Carol Smith
210–211:   Institute of Paleobiology, Warsaw, Poland*
212–213:   Robert Hynes
214–215:   Jim Pearson
216–217:   Colin Newman
218–219:   John Francis
220–221:   Samantha Carol Smith
222–223:   No. 315308, American Museum of Natural History*; Samantha Carol Smith
224–225:   Colin Newman
226–227:   ©Chip Clark*
228–229:   Bill Miller, photo by Ralph Brunke
230–231:   Gregory Paul; Roberta Polfus
232–235:   Gregory Paul
236–237:   Roberta Polfus; Larry Frederick
238–239:   Roberta Polfus
240–243:   Gregory Paul
244–247:   Jim Channell
248–249:   Bill Miller, photo by Ralph Brunke; Jim Channell
250–251:   Patricia Wynne
252–253:   John Rignall; Patricia Wynne
254–255:   John Rignall
256–257:   Patricia Wynne; Bill Miller, photo by Ralph Brunke
258–259:   John Rignall
260–263:   Kinuko Craft
264–265:   Edward Brooks
266–267:   Peter Barrett
268–269:   Edward Brooks
270–271:   John Rignall
272–273:   Edward Brooks
274–275:   Roberta Polfus
276–277:   Samantha Carol Smith
278–279:   Samantha Carol Smith; John Rignall
280–281:   Peter Barrett
282–283:   Phil Weare
284–285:   George Suyeoka, photo by Ralph Brunke
286–287:   Jennifer Emry-Perrott
288–289:   Phil Weare
290–291:   Jennifer Emry-Perrott
292–293:   Phil Weare
Size Comparisons: Zorica Dabich

Index

This index is an alphabetical list of the important topics covered in this book. It will help you find information given in both words *and* pictures. To help you understand what an entry means, there is often a helping word in parentheses. For example, ***Archaeopteryx*** (bird). If there is information in both words and pictures, you will see the words *with pictures* after the page number. If there is *only* a picture, you will see the word *picture* before the page number.